PEACEFUL BONES

The Inspiring Story of an Extraordinary Friendship During a Time of War, and the Heart-warming Reunion 46 Years Later That Captivated the World.

Captain Sam Axelrad M.D.

with Chris Axelrad and Rabbi Ranon Teller

Peaceful Bones

Printed in the United States of America

Scripture quotations marked (NKJV) are taken from the New King James Version®. Copyright © 1982 by Thomas Nelson. Used by permission. All rights reserved.

Scripture quotations marked (NIV) are taken from the THE HOLY BIBLE, NEW INTERNATIONAL VERSION®, NIV® Copyright © 1973, 1978, 1984, 2011 by Biblica, Inc.® Used by permission. All rights reserved worldwide.

Book design by Barbara Lindenberg, Bluebird Designs

ISBN: 978-0-692-79458-6

Dedicated to all the medics who
worked tirelessly to help save lives every day,
including the life of Hung Nguyen.

TABLE OF CONTENTS

FOREWORD

It was a hot July day in 2012 when I met Sam and his family at the Sofitel Metropole Hotel in Hanoi. I was working as a part-time "historian" at the five-star hotel—the most historic and classy hotel in the city.

I was doing it only on Saturday afternoons because I had a full-time job as an editor at a national daily newspaper in Vietnam. It was not because of the money but for the fun of being part of the legendary hotel built by the French in 1901.

My job was pretty simple, but it was very interesting. I took the Metropole's resident guests through the "path of history" tours of the hotel inside its premises. I explained to them about the ups and downs of the hotel throughout the country's war history and about the famous guests it once received. Charlie Chaplin, Jane Fonda, and Joan Baez were a few names among them.

At that time, the hotel ran four history tours a day with the last one wrapping up at around 7 p.m. I often stayed on to answer questions from the guests after the first three tours. Some of the chats were really interesting, as many of my guests were very knowl-edgeable. But often I left as soon as the last tour finished because it was time to get ready for dinner, and I was often pretty tired after four hours of continuous talking.

Sam and his family joined my last tour of that day. At the first place, I had a special feeling about these Americans. They were out-standing in the group with their interest. Even Sam's grandson, Ow-en—a very cute boy—was very smart and focused. After the tour con-cluded, I said good-bye to the guests and was excited to leave as usual. But Sam approached me and said, "I was in Vietnam during the war..."

All of a sudden, I forgot about my fatigue, thinking it would be interesting to stay on to talk to this gentleman and listen to his real experience about the wartime in Vietnam—something I, as a member of the post-war generation, only knew through books and my grand-parents' and parents' stories. I had met a few war vets in my previous tours, and they all brought their unique reflections to the conversa-tions. So I knew Sam's story would be another interesting one.

But it was far more than that ...

"I brought Charlie's arm bone back to the US and still keep it in a trunk ..."

I couldn't understand what Sam had said at first, partly be-cause I was not used to his Texas accent and partly because I would never imagine such a thing even in my dreams. I asked Sam again,

4

and I couldn't believe in my ears. I immediately thought about my position as a journalist.

I could probably be of some help, I told myself.

I said good-bye to Sam and his family after exchanging contact details with him. On the way back home, I planned to write a story about him and have it published with a fragile hope that Charlie or someone who knew him would read the message.

Sam's story was still on my mind after I got home that night. It was after 10 p.m. when I opened my laptop and tried to read Sam's email address from his handwritten note on the small piece of paper he gave me at the Metropole. I started to write to him:

Dear Sam,

This is Hoa from the Metropole. It was lovely to meet you and your family today. And it was great to hear your story …

Less than one hour after I clicked the "Send" button, Sam wrote me back. He promised to send me more information and some photographs when he returned to Houston.

Over the next weeks, we kept exchanging emails. I gained more details about his stories and also got in touch with Chris, his son, and one of Sam's former colleagues from the same company in

Vietnam during the war to build up the sources.

Then came the media-pitching task. I decided not to write the story for my newspaper—the national English daily publication—but targeted a popular Vietnamese tabloid, hoping that Charlie or his family would read the article.

As a journalist, it was not that difficult for me to get a helpful contact at the *Thanh Nien*, the second most widely read newspaper in the country, through a friend. An editor there told me to submit the story for her consideration.

However, this also came at a time when I had reached a crossroads in my career. I decided to leave my newspaper to join a UN organization in Vietnam. The application process and the start of the new job kept me fully occupied for about three months.

After I settled into the new post, I finished the story and submitted it to the *Thanh Nien* newspaper. Only a few hours later, I heard that they would use the article. It was good news but not so surprising to me, as I knew the story itself was interesting.

The story was finally published in November 2012. I sent a note to Sam in the US to keep him informed while praying for a miracle to happen. Usually, if the article could lead to something, you would know on the day the article was published or a few days after at the latest.

The first day went by without any news. My hope shrank a bit …

On the second day, I received an email from the newspaper—a reader wrote to them in response to my story. But it was not what I had been expecting.

The third day went by, and then the fourth day. It's over, I thought. I felt a little disappointed, even though I knew in advance that the chance of success was very small.

Five days after the story was published, I almost gave up hope altogether. It was a chilly Saturday, and it was also my birthday. I decided to run the tours at the Metropole as normal.

After the first two tours, I had a one-hour break. I turned on my phone to read through the congratulatory messages. But I saw several missed calls from the friend who used to work for the *Thanh Nien* newspaper and a brief text message from her: "Call me, he's found."

I called her back immediately and learned that the newspaper had found Charlie! Someone who knew him contacted the newspaper, and they were sending their correspondent to An Khe to confirm the news. I could not believe my eyes. This couldn't be true! Charlie was still alive!

I could not wait until I finished the fourth tour to inform Sam. I sent an email to my American friends just before I came back to work.

Dear Sam and Chris,

We found Charlie. He's still alive!

Congratulations!

What a wonderful gift I received for my birthday!

I soon received the contact details for Charlie—whose real name was Nguyen Quang Hung—from the Thanh Nien newspaper. Without any delay, I picked up the phone and called him immediately. My heart almost stopped beating in my chest when I heard the voice on the other end.

The conversation, however, was not what I expected because Charlie had a heavy south-central accent, whereas mine was typically Hanoian. Although I managed to get some key information, we had difficulties in understanding each other on the phone.

I asked him to write about his childhood, how he joined and served the North Vietnamese Army, and what happened to him after Sam left Vietnam. He was happy to do so and posted the letter to me. Charlie had never used any electronic means of communications before, so it was the only way I could get accurate information from him.

It took more than a week for his handwritten letter to reach me in Hanoi from the Central Highlands. It turned out that Charlie was still living in An Khe and had seven children, many of whom were university degree-holders.

While Sam was preparing for his return to Vietnam, I was thinking how amazing that story would be through the lens of journalism. Of course, it would be hot news for Vietnamese media, but it could be far more than that. Stories of former enemies' reuniting as long-lost friends had always made the headlines of Western media. And then there was the return of the arm bone.

So as soon as Sam and his family confirmed their trip—about three months out at that point—I spread the news to my international journalist friends who wrote for the AP, AFP, and VOA. As I expected, they replied immediately to my pitch email, asking for details. After that, it didn't take long for this extraordinary story to get out.

—*Tran Quynh Hoa*

INTRODUCTION

How the heck did anybody come out of here with their sanity? That's what I was thinking to myself, standing out near the Cu Chi tunnels in the middle of the Mekong Delta in South Vietnam.

It was the summer of 2012. My father, brother, nephew, and I were in Vietnam to look for Charlie, a North Vietnamese Army soldier my father had operated on in 1967 at a Forward Medical Command tent in the US Army's 1st Cavalry.

I knew from stories Dad had told me—and he didn't tell a whole lot of stories—that Charlie was someone very special to him. I first learned of Charlie when I was about ten years old, when I first heard the story of Dad's friend in Vietnam, a soldier he'd saved.

When he told me about Charlie, I sensed it was a special memory for him. I remember asking, "Where's Charlie now?"

"I don't know, Chris," Dad replied.

I was only ten, but I intuitively sensed Dad was feeling grief in that moment. And, honestly, I felt it, too. I wanted to meet Charlie. Even with the limited information I had about him, I knew he must have been special. And I sensed my father thought Charlie was probably dead.

So, I'm standing in the middle of this jungle in the Mekong Delta—a forty-three-year-old man on a journey with my seventy-four-year-old father back to Vietnam to look for Charlie. And it hits me … I fully understood how terrified everyone must have been back in 1967, when my father was there, when Charlie was there.

I am not pretending to have felt even one scintilla of the actual fear all those soldiers—on both sides—must have been feeling, walking through those jungles, wondering if their next step would be their last. Hearing explosions and gunshots in the distance or possibly even close by. Getting caught in an ambush by an enemy they couldn't see. Watching their friends suffering horrible wounds or even death right before their eyes.

It was almost as if I was time-traveling for a second. I was nineteen years old, walking through hell with an M16, fresh off the streets of my quiet little suburb in Houston, Texas.

It's a sort of strange twist that situations like that often bring out the best in people. And I really think that's what happened the day my father and Charlie met on that airstrip in South Vietnam in 1967.

As you see the story unfold for yourself, I think you'll understand why I feel the whole thing is full of miraculous moments. When you get past the political and social obstacles surrounding these two men—my dad and Charlie—it's a very human story.

I finally did meet Charlie. And, honestly, I think there's a special sincerity and humility about him. He has bravery and cleverness that not only allowed him to survive that terrible war but also to have an incredible, positive impact on so many lives both during and after it.

In the events of this story, two lives came together in the most horrifying and brutal place there is—an active war zone. From that moment, neither of them would ever be the same.

The way my father cared for Charlie may seem unbelievable. But anyone who knows Sam Axelrad knows that he takes care of his patients with all his effort. And that's the beauty of this whole story.

When Charlie came in and they laid his stretcher out on the ground and my dad looked at him in his broken state—in that moment Charlie wasn't a soldier.

He wasn't an enemy. He was a patient. He was a human being in need of healing.

And, heal Charlie did. As you'll read in this book, Charlie went on to help many, many people as both a medic and as a helpful companion during a war that was as misguided and pointless as it was brutal.

My dad always says that thinking back on this story—and all the events of his life that led up to it—he realized that "there are no accidents."

How right he is. To me, this story is not only about the amazing act of kindness and love my father completed by saving Charlie's life and finding him a safe place to live out the war. It is also about the fact that Charlie had a lot of life left to live, and he had a lot left to give.

It makes me sad to think of all those soldiers on both sides who didn't get out. All of them had more to live and more to give. Yet they died fighting a war that, in the end, everyone agrees would have been better left alone.

I'm glad Charlie made it. His is the ultimate survival story to me.

And that survival story—and the good that came out of it—wouldn't have been possible without the people, including my father and his medics, the helicopter pilot who picked Charlie up, and all those Americans and others who looked after him later. All of them knew his history. None of them turned him in or let their prejudices override their hearts.

All of them chose to put humanity before brutality, to find common ground in spite of conflict.

I hope, if nothing else, that you will be inspired by this book to do the right thing, to be kind, and to see the beautiful soul that is inside all people. Even those we call our enemy.

I am eternally grateful to have had this experience of searching for Charlie and then witnessing and participating in his reunion with my dad.

I want to make sure I give a very special and heartfelt thanks to Quynh Hoa, the Vietnamese journalist who we met in Hanoi on that first trip and who from the goodness and kindness of her heart took the time to listen to my father's story and then convince her editors to publish it on the front page of Thanh Nien. Hoa, you are a treasure, and the genuine kindness you displayed both in helping us find Charlie and then facilitating the reunion is something I will never forget. May you and your family be forever blessed.

— *Chris Axelrad*

PROLOGUE

My son Chris called me that morning, his voice brimming with excitement. I'd never heard him sound like that ... ever.

"Dad, you won't believe this. They found Charlie! They found him! He's still alive!"

Then he dropped an even bigger bombshell, "Not only is he alive, he's still living in An Khe Village where you left him all those years ago!"

A wave of relief overcame me. *Now, I can bring back his bones,* I thought.

Scenes I'd relived hundreds of times over the years played out again in my mind. I saw Charlie—Hung Nguyen to me then—as he'd been that first day, laid out on a stretcher in my med clinic, his arm so badly injured that I knew it would have to be amputated ... A healthier Charlie recovered and caring for others ... And my friend Charlie on the day we parted, when I'd left him at An Khe without a proper good-bye.

I had thought about him so often over the years, wondered what had happened to my enemy-turned-friend. He was still alive?

"How do you know?" I asked Chris.

"I just got an email from Hoa! Turns out Charlie's son-in-law saw her front-page article in that newspaper."

I was momentarily stunned, my mind spinning with this miraculous coincidence. You see, I'd recently taken a trip to Vietnam with my sons and grandson. I wanted them to see where I served during the war; I wanted them to meet the people I'd grown to respect and see the country I'd come to admire. During that trip, I'd tried unsuccessfully to find Hung Nguyen, the man I'd treated in 1967 when I was Captain in the 1st Air Cavalry's Forward Medical Company (which supported the 1st Brigade). He was a North Vietnamese soldier who became my friend, who we came to call "Charlie."

During our recent trip, a Vietnamese journalist, Hoa, wrote an article about my journey back to Vietnam with my two sons and grandson to find Charlie, and she managed to get it published on the front page of the newspaper, *Thanh Nien*. It included pictures of Charlie and me at LZ Hammond together. The now-famous picture of me shaking hands with Charlie, holding his left hand with my left hand, and the bones of his amputated right arm in my right hand; it was the biggest picture on the front page that day.

So his son-in-law in Ho Chi Minh City (formerly Saigon) saw the picture and knew immediately who it was. Of course, the fact that Hung only had one arm probably made this identification a little easier for him. And I'd like to think that just maybe Charlie had told his family the story about our care for him during the Vietnam War.

Apparently Hoa had already spoken to him for an interview to be published as soon as possible, again on the front page of the biggest newspaper in Vietnam. I was beside myself. I was amazed at how these events were lining up to help me find my old friend.

I replied to Hoa through my son Chris, and we requested a brief personal story of Charlie's life. All these years, I'd wondered what happened to him ...

You see, in order to keep him safe, I'd left him at a small US Army-supported Vietnamese medical clinic in 1967 in An Khe, where he was able to work as a clerk, translator, and medic.

When I had to leave suddenly at the end of my tour in 1967, I hardly had a chance to say good-bye. Needless to say, in the years that followed and as the war raged on and became the disaster we now know it to have been, I continually thought about Charlie and whether he was okay. He was a good man with a good heart.

A few days later, after she spoke with Charlie on the phone, Hoa sent over a transcript of her interview with him. This was never published in the paper. It was a personal story just for me.

Charlie's story represents the courage and dignity of the Vietnamese people during that horrible time of war—and this should not be overlooked. It is a human tendency to want to paint the world in black and white, "good guys" and "bad guys." But it is my sincere belief, as a Jew and as a human being, that there is good in all people and that deep down we share a common bond.

We, the Americans, may have thought we were saving them from the "evil empire" of communism. In the end, however, it was the courage and will of the Vietnamese people that prevailed over the massive military machine the US sent to destroy the communist movement sweeping through the country.

I remember something my son Chris said as we drove through the countryside on our trip; it's stuck with me to this day. "It's absolutely mind-blowing that these people stood up to the US and never backed down. It's a testament to the human spirit and how, in the end, guns and force never solve anything. They overcame our raw military might with love for their land and sheer willpower."

He was right. There wasn't a victory for anyone in the end. Yes, the Vietnamese people had defended their land, but at a staggering cost in both military and civilian life.

And we had left after losing so many great and brave soldiers on our side, in what turned out to be what I feel was a conflict needlessly escalated by inept politicians who had no idea what they were doing.

But, as with all trials and tribulations, there were victories to be had. And, in my opinion, those victories were in the stories of the ordinary people and soldiers who were there on the ground, doing their best to make a difference and do the right thing in the middle of absolute chaos and shameful violence.

I think it's fitting that we begin this book with Charlie's story because, honestly, he was the catalyst for so many lessons learned by myself and the troops under my command.

CHAPTER 1

Charlie's Story

I was born in 1939 to a farmer's family in Giao Thach Commune, Giao Thuy District, Nam Vinh province, about 150 kilometers southeast of Hanoi. I was the eldest in the family, two years senior to my sister and six years older than my brother.

My parents had quite a lot of land and rice fields, so we lived much better than many other people at that time. We were even listed as "rich farmers," who were always kept an eye on by the local authorities.

My parents' house was quite close to the sea, only two kilometers away. One of my uncles lived on fishing, so we always had lots of fish to eat at home.

When I was small, I dreamed of becoming a construction engineer one day. But I did not do well enough in school to make that dream come true. At that time, the school system had only ten grades, and once you completed Grade 7, you could switch to technical schools to learn a profession. I did that and spent another two years studying teaching methods to become a teacher.

But I never became a teacher either. I got my degree and was ready to work in 1964 when the war escalated. So, instead of starting my career in a classroom, I joined the army like many other young people in the country. The patriotic atmosphere was really high on every corner. Stories of heroes sacrificing themselves for the cause of independence were passing from people to people, calling on you to do something for the country.

In May 1965, I was first sent to the south. It took us about three months to move from Thanh Hoa province to Gia Lai province in the Central Highlands, all on foot.

It was such a fierce battle. Due to heavy death tolls, the northern army was short of advanced soldiers. So I enrolled in a non-commissioned officer candidate's course in 1966 before coming back to the battlefield as leader of an advanced squad.

Our team was ambushed when on mission one day later that year. Only I and another man survived, but I was shot in my right arm. We hid in a spring and followed the water for about four hours before reaching an abandoned village. The villagers eventually came back from the jungles at night. They gave us some rice and a blanket for me to cover myself. My companion used that little rice to cook porridge for us, and we survived in that way for three days. Meanwhile, the injury got worse due to the infection as a result of being in water for so long. My arm deteriorated and had a bad smell.

On the fourth day, we decided to carry on moving. When my companion and a villager were carrying me on a hammock, the American soldiers found us. They ran away, leaving me behind. I was so weak I did not really know what happened. Perhaps they took me in the hammock to a helicopter.

I eventually fainted when I reach the American medical site in Phu Cat. When I woke up, I found my right arm had been amputated. I knew the face of the surgeon who often came to check on me (Dr. Sam Axelrad), but I could not really remember his name. Western names were too difficult for me.

A few months later, I was brought to a clinic in An Khe where I worked as an assistant from 1966 to 1969. It was much to my surprise. I thought they would have me sent to Con Dao prison after I healed, but they did not.

In the first year, I was put under supervision by guards, but after a year, I was allowed to go out. I tried to get in touch with the northern army but failed to make contact. During my three years at the clinic, I learned about different types of medicine and how to take care of patients. This knowledge helped me a lot when I became a nurse after I left the clinic.

In 1969 when the American troops gradually left Vietnam, the clinic could not afford to have me there anymore and I was allowed to return to a local resettlement site.

A nurse who worked at the An Khe clinic really liked me and offered for me to come and live with his family, and I fell in love with his daughter who was fourteen years my junior—with his approval, of course. I must say it was my good luck. At that time, it was almost impossible for northerners to marry a local. So, I had my own family in 1971. After the war, I visited my family in Nam Dinh but could not tolerate the northern weather anymore. I decided to return to An Khe to settle down there.

I worked for the Song An commune administration in An Khe for several years then Chairman of the communal agricultural cooperative. I became self-employed in 1996 to feed my large family of seven children. I was proud to see five of them go to university or college, but it was a financial burden on us.

As time passed, my lost arm fell into oblivion. All of a sudden, I got it back from Dr. Axelrad who traveled all the way from the US with his family to reunite with me in 2013. There are no words to describe my tremendous happiness and gratitude toward Dr. Axelrad. He even *told me that if he had known my wife's sickness in advance, he would have brought her to the US so that she could have been treated.*

I have experienced the ups and downs of fate and seen many things in my life, but I was still speechless witnessing that miracle. He was an American doctor, and I was only a prisoner; ours was not a normal relationship. The way he treated me was full of love and sympathy. If I had been in his position, I would not have done the same thing. Now in my seventies, I have been taught a new lesson about love of mankind.

~

As I read and reread this transcript, I began to reflect back on my early life.

What was it that led me to join the army, how did I end up in the 1st Cavalry as the commander of a Forward Medical Hospital? How did I end up there that day when Hung was brought to our base on a US helicopter gunship? And what influenced me to go to such great lengths to save, help, and guide an enemy soldier in a time of war?

I now know that these influences and experiences were guided from above by the Creator of the Universe. There is no way I just "happened" to be there. Simply put, there are no accidents.

CHAPTER 2

The Journey Back to Vietnam

In 2012, I decided to return to Vietnam with my two sons—Chris and Larry—and my grandson Owen. It was important to me to share this experience with them. My daughter had an infant son at the time, so she couldn't go with us.

We left at the end of June 2012, and we arrived in Vietnam the first week of July 2012. We toured the country from the bottom to the top—from Mekong Delta to Ha Long Bay to Hanoi. We had a guide in each of three major sections of the country—the south, middle, and north.

To read about our trip in detail, visit my son Chris's blog. It outlines our trip and includes many amazing photos, which can be found here: www.peacefulbones.com.

Sitting in a plane, flying over Vietnam, I thought back a couple of years to a moment that foreshadowed this trip. Owen sat with me in my study one day and asked, "Saba (a Jewish term for grandfather), what is in the red, white, and blue trunk?"

"I'm not sure," I told him.

"Can we open it?" he asked with that childlike curiosity.

"Sure, Owen, let's see what's in there."

I'd kept that trunk closed for over forty years. Honestly, I wasn't sure I was ready to deal with what was inside. But when your grandson makes a request like that with such sincerity, how do you say no?

So we opened the trunk. It was filled with documents and keepsakes: orders, travel tickets, newspaper articles, and about 140 color slides. But there was one item that stood out, to say the least. It was a gray plastic bag containing something you don't see every day.

Inside that plastic bag were the bones of Charlie's amputated right arm; they were intact and wired together. The medics in my company had been so moved by my gesture of saving that NVA soldier's life all those years ago, they had taken the arm, reconstructed the bones, and given them to me as a token of their appreciation for what I'd done.

At that moment, I remembered putting the bones in my trunk for safekeeping, intending to give them back to Hung (aka "Charlie") as soon as he was recovered from his terrible injuries. But the chaos of war would have it otherwise. In the haste with which I had to get Charlie off the base, I didn't have time to think about giving him the bones. To be honest, I'd all but forgotten they were there as I moved around to locations all across the Vietnamese countryside on various medical assignments.

"Wow, Saba, what is this?" Owen exclaimed.

I explained to him the basics of the story—that a soldier had been brought to our base with a very serious injury to his arm, and I'd had to amputate it.

"Is he still alive?" Owen asked.

I paused. "Honestly, Owen, I don't know … but I'm sure going to find out."

It was that moment that I knew I was going to return to Vietnam to find that soldier, that North Vietnamese soldier who'd changed my life and the lives of so many of the other troops I worked with over there.

I simply had to know what happened to him and, at the very least, return the bones to his family. I suspected that he hadn't survived the war, but I needed to know for certain

I did not intentionally keep those bones. They were never a trophy of war or a souvenir. The bones had been given to me as a gesture of appreciation by the medics on my team. The brutality of war was taking a toll on all of us. It may be difficult for someone who's never served in a war to understand why the medics did what they did by reconstructing those arm bones and giving them to me.

What they did was a form of therapy, a symbol of appreciation because we'd helped an enemy soldier instead of sending him off to be slaughtered. We'd saved a life instead of taking it. They wanted to commemorate that somehow. They wanted to witness that moment of kindness that we'd all participated in.

So, I knew that moment I was going back to Vietnam. I just knew. I started looking over the photographs that I developed from the slides. Well ... that sealed the deal.

I hadn't thought much about my war experiences since leaving Vietnam. Honestly, I didn't want to think about them. But as I looked at those pictures, foggy memories returned. Over time, I started remembering more and more. I felt compelled to do more research.

I read the speech that Lyndon Johnson gave to Congress. I read the speech that Secretary of State Dean Rusk gave to Congress. I obtained a history of the 1st Cavalry from the 1st Air Cavalry Association. The year that I was there—1966 to 1967—was specifically reviewed, and as it turned out, my medical company supported 80% to 90% of the 1st Cavalry's combat missions in Vietnam for seven months. I never knew that. I obtained a book written by H.R. McMaster, a major general in the army today. The book was about the secret documents of the Lyndon Johnson administration that had become public in the years 1986 to 1987. The book also included a discussion on the relationship between Johnson and his secretary of defense, McNamara, who was a major influence in Johnson's decisions.

After reviewing the research material, looking over the photographs, and discussing it further with Owen, I began planning in earnest my return to Vietnam with my two sons and grandson. I needed to share this history with them. I needed to travel to Vietnam with them to share the story of this time in my life. I needed to find Charlie, return the bones, and make things whole again. I needed closure. I needed peace.

CHAPTER 3

Back Where It All Began

More than twenty hours into our journey, the boys and I got off the plane in Ho Chi Minh City. We spent the first two weeks of July 2012 touring the country from the Mekong Delta to Ha Long Bay.

In the Mekong Delta, we rode bikes, walked along pathways, and visited the underground tunnels. We even took a boat ride along the Delta. Then we flew to several sites including An Khe—the village where it turned out Charlie was living all this time—to Quy Nhon, a small town along the coast where I remembered that the army had a hospital.

We stayed in a very nice hotel, and the beaches were magnificent. When we got to An Khe, we drove over to the area where my base camp had been located. It was called Camp Radcliff. After the war, the camp was transformed into a major army base for the Vietnamese army, so we couldn't get too close.

We were in the area, but the sites were unfamiliar to me. When I was there, the area had been totally cleared. Today, there are trees and plants covering the ground. It was a verdant, fertile place now—not the desolate, flat, and dusty airstrips I remembered.

It had been close to fifty years since I stood in those places. The transformation was incredible. We also visited Hon Cong Mountain, a large hill in the center of Camp Radcliff where I'd been stationed. Again, we were not allowed to go up to the area where you could see the base camp.

I remember all the guns and cannons and all the communication systems that were on that mountain. It was totally secure because the mountain was impenetrable to any motor attack. And since the Vietnamese did not have any aircraft, it was safe from above.

We also went 50 miles north of Quy Nhon and visited Phu Cat. Then, we went north of the city of Phu Cat to LZ (Landing Zone) Hammond, which was where I'd stayed for over six months. There is a lot of history there for me. As I stood there again almost fifty years later, memories became more clear and present.

My thoughts went to the Marine areas where I'd experienced some very difficult things. I started to remember all the children I'd seen in our field hospital, and how many of them were orphaned or simply unable to find their parents. I remembered the men I'd served with. I remembered the ones I'd been able to save, and I remembered the ones who didn't make it or were dead on arrival.

All these thoughts and memories were racing through my mind as I stood there in Vietnam all those years later. I was glad that my sons and grandson were there with me. Later I found myself getting emotional at seeing their reaction to the unfolding events of our trip.

I was also experiencing moments of sadness. I was actually missing my troops. I spent a lot of time wondering about where they were today and whether they were still living or had passed away. I pray that they've had a good life.

CHAPTER 4

There Are No Accidents

All these events had me thinking about how I met Charlie in the first place. What force guided me to that place and time? I realized I'd have to go as far back as the early days when my grandfather came to the United States.

My grandfather, Souza Axelrad, came through the Port of Galveston from Bukovina, Romania, in 1907. As many immigrants did at that time, he'd left his wife and six children behind in Europe while he got himself established in the United States.

There were four boys and two girls. He worked for about five years, and then he sent for his eldest son. His eldest was turning thirteen and was about to be drafted into the Austrian army. The family was able to get him on a boat, and he came to the United States to be with his father. The rest of the family came several years later through the port in Baltimore, and they settled in Houston, Texas. Then one daughter went to California.

That was my Aunt Molly, or "Aunt Doc" as we affectionately called her. She was probably the first female dentist in the State of Texas, and I know for sure she was one of the first female oral surgeons and had training all over the world.

Her life was rather extraordinary and eccentric, to say the least, but she was incredibly gifted. She lived with her husband, and she had a female lover who ran her dental office. Incidentally, she was Orson Welles' dentist. She would travel to New York City and stay at the Waldorf Astoria Hotel. There, she became friendly with many of the Broadway stars at the time.

One of my grandfather's first jobs was as a coppersmith when Rice Institute (now called Rice University) was built. He lived in a residential neighborhood on Preston Avenue, in what is now downtown Houston, and rode a horse-drawn trolley to his job every day.

He was also a good carpenter and builder. He opened a hardware store on Lyons Avenue on the outskirts of downtown. When the Jewish people came to Houston from Eastern Europe, they all knew to go to the Axelrad Hardware Store, where they would get help from my grandfather. He would find them a job and a place to live.

The small stores at that time had sleep areas upstairs or in the back, and oftentimes the owners would sleep in the store at night. But when they didn't sleep there, they would always keep an extra bed just in case.

My grandfather became an important leader of the Houston Jewish community. Many of these immigrants became rich and wealthy, and their descendants don't know their own family history about how they came to Houston and stayed with Mr. Axelrad in his hardware store.

My maternal grandfather owned a dry goods store in Miami, Florida, that was completely wiped out in a hurricane in 1926. He had no means of making a living, so he decided to move to Houston from Miami to find work to support his family.

Like everyone else, he was told to go to the Axelrad Hardware Store. But instead of going to my grandfather's store, he went to my father Jack's store instead.

My father, Jack Harry Axelrad, also had a hardware store on McKinney Avenue in the middle of downtown, which ended up being a very important turn in my personal history, as you'll soon see.

My father put him up in his store, and that is where he stayed. He had left his family in Miami to be brought to Houston by a hired driver who would drive their car.

As the rest of his family was en route from Miami, something unexpected happened. About 90 miles into their journey, the driver simply disappeared. He'd been paid half up front, and I guess he'd decided that was enough for him. Apparently his plan all along was to steal the money.

My grandmother barely spoke English, and she certainly couldn't drive a car. Her daughter, my future mother, took the wheel.

My mother, Sylvia Rosen, was only sixteen years old at that time. Stuck outside Miami with her mother and three younger siblings, having barely driven before, Sylvia did something bold that would foreshadow many things to come for her—she took the wheel of that car and drove all the way to Houston. At that time, it was at least a two or three day trip!

After this, she became the head of the family and helped them integrate into the Houston community.

A few years later, her father died. His name was Samuel Daniel Rosen, for whom I was named. He had some type of skin condition, and after staying with my father, he moved from Houston to Galveston with his family to be in the sun more often, which was good for his skin.

While he was there, he got a bowel inflammation and had surgery at St. Mary's Hospital and died from complications in 1927.

So, there was my mother—now seventeen years old—with

three younger siblings and a mother who was basically illiterate. She became the sole means of support to take care of that family.

They moved back to Houston and reconnected with my father, who continued to help them out. And that is how my parents met—when her father came to my father's hardware store by "accident." I count this as one of the first of many "accidents" leading to my meeting with Charlie.

My father wanted to marry my mother but, like any good Jewish woman, she had stipulations—the primary one being that he had to become a lawyer. So, he got himself a tutor and studied for the bar exam. Back then you didn't have to complete law school to become a lawyer, you only had to pass the bar. He passed the bar examination on his first attempt and became a licensed attorney in the State of Texas. So my mother agreed to marry him.

I was born on September 2, 1938. My brother Moise was five years older than me. My younger brother, David, came four years later, and my sister, Sandra, three years after him. My mother had four children, and each time she had a child, she developed toxemia and was told not to have another child. But, as was the norm for Sylvia, she didn't listen to the doctors. Every time they'd tell her to stop and, after three or four years, she would have another child.

Because of her history of toxemia, she remained in the hospital for a while after each birth and came home when she recovered.

After I was born, I was sent home with my father and had a brit mi-lah—a ritual circumcision conducted at eight days old. Apparently, my mother was discharged right before the brit milah, and they gave me the name Samuel Daniel Axelrad.

As a side note, I never liked the name Daniel. Years later when I got through high school, I took on the name Donald in place of Daniel. And, hence, Samuel Donald Axelrad was the name on my certificates from junior high school, college, medical school, and the military. At the time my first son, Chris, was born in 1969 (after my service in Vietnam), I was a resident at Baylor. Because I had a child, I was entitled to an extra $70.00 per month from the army as part of the G.I. Bill. So I went down to the City Health Department and got a copy of Chris's birth certificate. While I was there, I decided to get my own. When they handed me the birth certificate, much to my surprise, it said "Baby Boy Axelrad." For all these years, that had been my actual legal name! Because of my mother's toxemia and her rush to get home for my circumcision ceremony, she never complet-ed my birth certificate at the hospital. So my name was never offi-cially submitted to the Health Department. Right then and there, I officially gave myself the name Samuel Donald Axelrad. I was twen-ty-nine years old.

From the time I was a child, we lived on Hutchins Street in Houston. It was a duplex that my father built himself. All the boys slept in one room, and then my sister had a room of her own.

My father built all the toys we had. There was no such thing as going to a store and buying toys. My father made kites and rubber guns. He even built me a scooter out of old roller skates. It wasn't pretty, but it worked.

Our house was off McGowen street, not far from downtown Houston. For allowance, my brother Moise would get twenty-five cents and I would get ten cents. That's all we needed to go to the Sunset Movie Theatre on McGowen every Saturday afternoon. The movie ticket would cost nine cents. Since Moise had another fifteen cents, he could get a Coke and a bag of popcorn. But I came up with a solution. Since I only had ten cents to get into the movie, I would go around the neighborhood, pick up Coke bottles, and take them to the local grocery store where they would give me two cents apiece. I earned an extra twenty or thirty cents.

When I got to the movie theater, I had enough money to buy a Coke, a bag of popcorn, and a bar of candy! I never complained to my parents. I never quite understood why Moise got twenty-five cents and I only got a dime, but I never let it stop me from working toward my goal.

When we lived on Hutchins, summertime was special. All the kids on the block would go barefoot and wear short pants and a T-shirt. I wore the same pair of blue short pants the whole summer.

It was only later that I learned that my mother would wash the pants at night and iron them.

For the Fourth of July, my father would take us to my grandfather's hardware store, where he had firecrackers stored in his storage area. Because there was a fireworks factory in Houston, everybody in the neighborhood had access to fireworks. One day, the fireworks factory blew up and caused a fire on the whole block, and that ended fireworks in Harris County. After the factory exploded, in order to get the fireworks you had to go to the county border, buy from sale trucks, bring them back into the county to celebrate the Fourth of July.

One time, I threw a little firecracker on the ground, and my brother David picked it up and it exploded. It caused burns on his hands and fingers, and he had to be taken to St. Joseph Hospital, where they dressed the burn.

It is interesting that my sister, Sandra, later put her hand on a hot iron. She burned her hand to the point that she had to have skin grafts in order for her to have mobility of her fingers. It was a terrible thing. She didn't let it slow her down, though. In her teen years, she became a dancer and performer. In her adult life, she received a Master of Fine Arts and then a fellowship in children's theater at Frank Lloyd Wright's Kalita Humphreys Theater in Dallas. When she returned to Houston, she worked as a theater arts teacher for the Houston School District. To this day, I run across her former students who remember her fondly.

We lived on the corner and the ice skating rink was across the street and the icehouse was down the street from there. Further down the street was a potato chip factory. The manager would let me and the neighborhood kids in with a little bag, and we could catch the potato chips as they were coming off the conveyor belt. We played baseball on the gravel parking lot of the ice skating rink and, of course, I went ice skating probably three nights a week until I was nine or ten years old. I became a very good skater.

We moved from Hutchins Street to Binz in 1949, across from the Schlumberger estate. I used to go over to their house and play with the kids. That's where I taught myself how to swim. Sammy Schlumberger owned the Schlumberger companies, a worldwide leader in oil drilling and production. Next door to them was the Ben Taub estate. Ben was a multimillionaire and a key player in the development of the Texas Medical Center, including the county hospital, which is now named Ben Taub Hospital in his memory.

As I thought about these and other memories from my childhood, I couldn't help returning to my war experience. I'm sure I'm not the only one who feels this way, but it just seems so incredible that a boy like me—growing up going to the skating rinks and movie theaters—a little Jewish boy whose grandfather had come from so far away, ended up where I did, in such a faraway place myself, amid such chaos.

CHAPTER 5

Horses and Cavalries

remember Saturday afternoons when I was eleven years old. All the kids would hop on their bicycles and head toward Almeda Street to go to the Almeda Theater. We were all going to the theater to see the cartoons and to watch a children's movie. One time, on the way to the movies, I stopped off at the Almeda Stables about a block before the movie theater. After that, I was at the stables every day for the next three years.

I discovered the horses and they became my life's passion. The owner of the stables accepted me unconditionally. I was incredibly lucky that I had visited the stables that day ... accidentally.

It changed my life. Incidentally, I ended up in the 1st Cavalry, which was the original horse-mounted division of the US Army. There are no accidents.

It seemed like a miracle that not only did I never have to pay to ride a horse again, I was actually paid to ride them. I never owned a horse, but horse owners kept asking me to show their horses at the shows.

I rode jumping horses, drove hayrides in the park, worked cattle, and cared for the horses when they were ill. It was a rather unusual experience for a young teenager in general, but being a Jewish boy from the Southeast part of Houston, trust me, this was nothing short of a miracle. Jewish boys were preparing to be doctors, lawyers, and businessmen—not horse trainers and jockeys.

At the stables, we organized hayrides every Friday and Saturday night. Most of the time, they were for children and teenage kids who were having their birthday parties. My job was to take them for a ride in the park. Then they would get out of the wagon and go into the pavilion to have a birthday party. They would eat birthday cake and roast marshmallows on the fire pit. After the party was over, we would put the kids back into the wagon and bring them back to the stables.

Sometimes the owner of the stables would ask me to go out to a ranch to round up cattle. There was a gentleman who had several thousand acres of rice land and rice dryers. He had large herds on his ranch. Our job was to round up the cattle and bring them in so they could separate the calves from the mothers. These calves were sold off. It was an amazing and unique experience. Sometimes, we would bring the cows and the calves toward the barn where a milk cow was tied to the fence. The milk cow was meant to be a lead cow to bring the cows and calves in. The idea was that the herd would follow the cow.

But every once in a while, one of the bulls would swing around, shake his tail, and take off. Then the herd would swing around and take off after the bull. We would have to round them up again and bring the whole herd back to the barn. Sometimes we did that as many as three times, and it would take all day to get the herd into the barn.

When I was fourteen years old and just starting the tenth grade, I was about 5 feet 11 inches, weighed 127 pounds, and I was training three jumping horses. The horses that I trained were ridden through the park in the morning and then jumped at night. I was getting more and more involved with the horses, and I was not doing very well in school.

My parents were getting somewhat disturbed, as my life was not going exactly the way they wanted it to go. My mother, who ended up raising three physicians and an educator, was not happy to see me spending so much time in the park with horses. I was earning one dollar an hour, and I was saving my money in the Almeda State Bank. When I saved enough money, I spent it on riding boots. I knew my parents didn't like me spending so much time with the horses, so I tried to keep my riding activities secret from them. But they knew what I was doing. I was enjoying it so much, I just didn't want them to stop me. I remember one special horse, her name was Candy, and she was my show horse. I took her to several horse shows, and I won many ribbons riding her.

One of my talents at the stables was the ability to simultaneously ride and soothe a horse. This was part of my own instinctive training method. The other instructors and the owners had never seen anything like it. For me, riding these horses was almost like a hypnotic experience. I have since learned that there is a field of psychotherapy that uses horses to help people cope with stress. Equine therapy is a very important method used for children with autism. It is also being used for military veterans who have posttraumatic stress syndrome. So, in hindsight, for me those horses were therapy.

I remember one of the horses most vividly. His name was Rocket. Rocket was a Palomino stallion, and so he was aggressive, particularly in front of crowds. I trained him, but I did not show him. The stables hired a professional rider to show him because he was really difficult to control in front of large crowds. But he was a champion horse, and he was exceptional. Rocket generally had to be separated from the other horses, but when we traveled and had limited space, he was kept in the trailer with the other horses. It is a small miracle that the other horses survived the trip.

The next "accident" that played a big part in my journey to becoming a captain of a medical battalion in Vietnam happened that same year.

The owner of the stable left me in charge of the hayrides. He instructed me to take the hayride from 9:00 to 12:00 and instructed my friend Bobby to take the 6:00 to 9:00 group. But when he left, I switched it. I took the 6:00 to 9:00 group to the park and brought them back. Bobby left at nine o'clock with a fresh team of horses. Suddenly at eleven o'clock, I was sitting there and waiting for him to return, and I saw Bobby walking across the ring, smoking a cigarette and laughing.

I said, "Bobby, where are the kids?" He replied that they were in the pavilion.

I said, "Where are the horses?"

He said, "They're in the park."

I said, "Where's the wagon?"

He said, "It's up a tree."

Bobby dropped off the kids around the campfire. Then, just as he was tying the horses to a tree, a car backfired and made a pop like a firecracker! The horses took off toward the tree and, sure enough, the wagon went up a tree. The harness and chains broke, and the horses ran wild into the park.

It was pouring rain. Bobby and I got on horseback, and we rode through the park all night long until we found the horses. To this day, I do not know how the kids from the birthday party got home. We found one horse wrapped up in the harness, but he was okay. The other horse was picked up by dogcatchers! After riding in the rain all night, I got pneumonia. I was not taking care of myself in general. My body was wearing thin. I kept an extensive horse-training schedule, worked the hayrides, tried to keep all this secret from my parents, and still went to school all day. The pneumonia was pretty bad, so bad that I had to drop out of high school. My uncle, who was an internist, came to the house, told me that I had TB, and ordered me to stay in bed for thirty days.

Looking back on it, I think he had a conspiracy with my parents to keep me away from the horses and regain my health.

My family had a maid named Viola, and every day for thirty days she fed me steak and calf's liver. Then my uncle came over with raw cow's milk from his farm. I gained a pound a day for thirty days, and by the end I weighed 157 pounds. I had been away from the stables for a month.

When I recovered, I returned to school and started making

A's and B's. Instead of spending time at the stables, I joined a Jewish youth group called Abe Silverman AZA. I enrolled at Lamar High School and made up an entire half grade. Then I made A's and B's in summer school.

In the meantime, my mother and father had been making plans to send me to military school. When they saw that I had rehabilitated myself, was doing well in school, and had good friends, they gave me an option. I could either continue the good work I was doing now, staying away from the stables, or I could sign up at Sewanee Military Academy in Tennessee.

I was at a crossroads. For whatever reason, I felt guided to go to military school. Later, it became clear why God had guided me in that direction. When I became the commanding officer of a medical company in Vietnam in the 1st Air Cavalry division, it was my military school experience, my equine experience, along with my medical education, that gave me standout qualifications for becoming a unit commander.

Sewanee Military Academy in Tennessee was a historic Deep South military academy that went back to the Civil War. The physicians in the community were the Edmund Kirby Smith family who were descendants of the Confederate general by the same name.

They kept us on a rigorous schedule. At six o'clock in the morning, we were awakened by the bugle over the loudspeaker. We got out of bed and went outside in formation, for the headcount until everyone was present and accounted for. Then we would go back to our rooms, take a shower and shave, and clean our rooms to military perfection.

While we were in class, one of the inspector teachers would inspect our rooms and hand out demerits if anything was out of place. If we had too many demerits, we had to report on our free afternoon and march back and forth on the huge platform on campus. Two hours of marching worked off two demerits.

For those of us who were honor students, we earned the privilege to go to a movie in town on our free Wednesday afternoons. It was not a big movie theater—essentially only a room with a projector in the back—but the movies were current. If you didn't go to the movies, you could run the hills up toward the edge of the mountain and get in some extra exercise.

There were very high academic requirements at the Academy. Classroom instruction was over by noon. Then we went into formation and marched into a mess hall for our lunch. Every afternoon, we had ROTC classes and drill teams with sports activities.

I went out for the drill team. At football games, we would march and do special drill formation. It was really fun and took a lot of discipline, but it was a good group of guys, and we did the best we could.

The other advantage of being on the drill team was that we

would be invited to communities in Tennessee and Alabama to march in special parades. When we went to these communities, the local Episcopal Church would have a party for us where there were girls from the local town. Then whenever we had dances in Sewanee, we would invite the girls that we had met to the mountain.

The girls would stay in the faculty homes. There was a curfew, but it was a lot of fun for a group of guys who were in the disciplined situation of a military academy.

Every Sunday morning at nine o'clock, the students would get into formation and march into Sewanee, where the entire community would be standing up in front of the All Saints' Chapel. When the band started playing "Onward Christian Soldiers," the entire community lifted up in song. We would go into the chapel first, and the community would follow.

Going to Sewanee was a good decision. I know I was meant to be there. My two years of training there helped me later when I found myself in combat situations. I was proud to be a student in the 1956 graduating class. I graduated with honors, and so I was automatically accepted to both Tulane University and Vanderbilt University. But I wanted to go home, so I chose to go the University of Texas instead.

CHAPTER 6

One Step Closer to Army Surgeon

I n 1956, I went to the University of Texas in Austin. My four years there were a great experience. I had my share of girlfriends and became the president of my fraternity. The president was called the Master of the Fraternity.

I worked hard and did the best I could. I even had a decent grade point average at the end of four years.

Before I graduated, I wanted to take an advanced physiology course. It was Physiology 385. When I got to the class, it turned out that it was a special class for the football team. I was the only non-athlete there. In any case, I finished the class with a 97 average.

The star running back sat to my right, real close, and wouldn't you know—he made the same grade I did! Then one of the star linemen sat behind me, also kind of close, and he got the same grades, too! The entire football team was in formation around me.

When the school year was over, I would get back to Houston for the summers, but I never returned to the stables. My riding days were over.

My uncle had a farm about thirty miles outside of Houston, and I would raise calves there. First I would buy a milk cow and then I would buy two newborn calves. My milk cow would accept and raise these calves. So, in the end I had four cows and twelve calves. These cows were my summer project all the way through college.

When it was time to apply to medical school, I had a very crucial intuitive, almost telepathic experience.

Before I tell that story, I'm remembering another telepathic moment I haven't mentioned yet about when my father passed away. I knew it had happened before I heard the news.

I was 19 years old; I was asleep in my apartment in Austin and suddenly I woke up, literally falling off the bed. I looked up at the clock, and it was exactly midnight. For some reason, I remembered that time. I had an intuitive sense that something had happened to my father.

I subsequently found out the next morning that my father

had a massive heart attack and died at midnight—at the exact same time I'd looked at the clock.

It was one of the saddest days of my life.

Then years later, I was playing canasta with some friends across from my mother's apartment, and I had a sudden thought that I needed to go home. I had been put on a waitlist for medical schools, and a week before school was supposed to start I still hadn't gotten in. I was expecting a phone call from the school about my admission sometime in the range of those few weeks.

The minute I walked into my mother's apartment, the phone rang, and it was the Dean of Medicine at the University of Texas Medical Branch in Galveston, informing me that I had been accepted and that I needed to show up the next day for class.

The next morning, I was on the road to Galveston. That was how my medical career began. If I hadn't responded to my intuition, I may never have been in the medical school. God has been guiding me every step on my journey.

I arrived in Galveston, enrolled in medical school, and joined one of the fraternities, which was where I lived for the next four years.

After my second year in school, I was home for the summer. My brother David came up to the apartment and said, "You know, there's a pretty girl out there by the swimming pool. You should go meet her." And, I said to him, "Well, David, why are you coming to get me? How come you don't go meet her?"

I went out by the pool and saw this pretty girl—Charlotte Senger—sitting at one of the tables, playing cards. Charlotte later became my wife. She had arrived from Milwaukee, Wisconsin, after high school and, at the encouragement of her mother, enrolled at St. Mary's Nursing School in Galveston to get her certificate as a registered nurse.

During my senior year in medical school, as I was applying for an internship, I did something rather unusual. I took a train from Houston all the way to Boston, stopped in Washington, DC, Pennsylvania, New York City, and Boston. I visited several hospitals and training programs throughout my travels. While I was in Philadelphia, I decided to take the train to Washington, DC, and visit a couple of my friends who were at DC General Hospital as interns. They had graduated a year ahead of me in Galveston. In Washington, I interviewed at DC General Hospital, Georgetown Medicine, and subsequently became an internal medicine intern at DC General Hospital.

I remember when I selected the program, I sent a letter to the physician who was the chief of the internship. I explained to him that I was placing his program as my number one choice, and I would appreciate it if he would give me the privilege of having a match to become one of the house staff officers at DC General Hospital.

And it worked.

I drove to Washington, DC, and lived in the staff dormitory on the same property as the DC General Hospital.

As a side note, the hospital was situated next to the National Cemetery, where the second and third presidents of the United States are buried. This area of town was not very safe, though, and tourists generally stayed away.

My original intention was to become a cardiologist. The number one cardiologist in the world was nearby at Georgetown University Hospital, and he was an amazing teacher and physician. Every Thursday night, he had a conference at Georgetown and 300 to 500 physicians would show up every week. On one Thursday night a month, he would take the program to one of the peripheral hospitals.

At that time, the military draft was in full swing. College students received a deferment, and then served in active duty upon graduation. Most of my friends in college joined ROTC, so when they graduated, they went in as officers rather than enlisted men.

However, the pre-med students did not take ROTC in college. When you were accepted to medical school, you were given an automatic four-year deferment to complete your education, and you were given an additional year of deferment to complete the internship.

Therefore, during my internship, I applied for another three to four-year deferment in order to be assured of a residency. But I was only given one year.

So, subsequent to my internship, I went into a one-year residency in general surgery at Georgetown University Hospital since I was not able to get a residency in internal medicine. My first rotation there was in Urology. The professor's name was Roger Baker, and I was completely blown away by him. The residents were also fantastic, and that is the reason I became a urologist.

The professor allowed me to primarily take care of children, which I was glad to do. He also allowed me the specialty care for men and women of all ages. My medical internship gave me the background to do primary care urology. Urology is surgical, but there is a lot of primary care with regard to general medicine.

My internship started in July of 1964, and by November of that year, I was given an appointment as a Reserve Commissioned Officer as a first lieutenant.

I reported to Fort Holabird, Maryland, where I spent the day to be sworn in as a Reserve Officer. On December 16, 1965, I received orders from Fort Meade, Maryland, that included information on my active duty commitment.

Then on May 7, 1966, I received my orders for active duty and my assignment to the 1st Infantry Division in Vietnam. I was instructed to appear at Fort Sam Houston and sign in to the military on July 5, 1966.

I attended the Medical Field Service School at Brooke Army Medical Center at Fort Sam Houston. On August 6, 1966, I received a certificate that I had completed my training at Brooke Army Medical Center with about two hundred other physicians, and then on August 11, 1966, I was on my way to Vietnam.

CHAPTER 7

How I Suddenly Became the Captain of a Medical Company

After graduating from Fort Sam Houston Medical Field Service School and just before heading out to Vietnam, I returned home for several days to visit family. Then I flew from Houston Hobby Airport to San Francisco. I remember my entire family was at the airport when I left: my brother Moise, my sister Sandra, my mother, and my then-girlfriend and future wife Charlotte.

It felt strange and lonely to be leaving them and going off to war. It was a sad moment. But I also sensed profound love and affection from everybody. And so it was also a moment of deep inspiration. It just seemed right. It's hard to explain, but somehow I knew I was in the right place at the right time.

I traveled to San Francisco, and from San Francisco I took a cab to the Travis Air Force Base and checked in. As I departed from Travis Air Force Base into international territory, I still remember the feeling that I was traveling into the complete unknown. For the first time since getting my orders to go to Vietnam, I was scared.

From Travis Air Force Base, I flew to Anchorage, Alaska, for a one-hour layover, then off to Japan. Along the Alaskan coast the pilot flew at about 10,000 feet so he could point out the glaciers and other geological features along the way. It was truly awesome.

In Japan, we landed at the American air base and sat in the plane for two hours. From there, we flew directly to Saigon Tan Son Nhut Air Base. I was there for three days, then flown to the 1st Cavalry base camp.

When I landed on the air base, I stood frozen on the landing strip. I looked out at the sea of helicopters and military aircraft. The base was huge, and in the center of the base was the helicopter line-up base and the airstrip. The setup made it impossible for a mortar round to reach the aircraft from the perimeter.

The landing zone was near a small mountain, now known as Hon Cong Mountain. On the top of that mountain, I took in all the communication systems and the artillery weapons used to protect the perimeter.

The mountain had its own special crane helicopter, which was a heavy-equipment moving apparatus, and it ferried all types of equipment to the top of that mountain. The equipment was used to flatten the surface of the mountain for artillery and the other military weapons.

At Tan Son Nhut Air Base I was informed that I would be delayed three or four days. When I arrived in Saigon, I was told to wait for further orders, and I was at Saigon at the Tan Son Nhut Base for about three days. The waiting was challenging, and the weather there in August was extremely hot and incredibly humid. Of course, growing up in Houston I had a lifetime of training for the heat and humidity.

I hung out at the officer's club, mainly because the club was air-conditioned. Then I received orders to travel by C130 from Saigon to the base camp near An Khe.

An Khe is about 36 miles west of the Port City of Quy Nhon. The moment I arrived at the base camp of the 1st Cavalry Division, I was taken to the division headquarters, where I met the division sergeant, and he assigned me to Company A in the 15th Medical Battalion.

This medical company was designed to be a forward surgical hospital. I was taken to the company area, where the commanding officer was in his tent. He never came out. And so, I met with First Sergeant John Jones and Executive Officer William Boyd.

In retrospect, it's clear that they were checking me out to potentially become the new company commander. At the time, I was totally unaware that there were plans to make me the commanding officer of that entire unit. It was strange that the current commander stayed down in his hooch, and I never even saw the man or met him in the two-week overlap that he and I were there at the same time.

I guess I passed their test, because a week later I was given the orders. I was to become the company commander of this unit. There were about 130 enlisted men, which included the non-commissioned officers. The company had seven officers. Four of us were physicians, and the other three were administrative officers, including Executive Officer William Boyd.

Then there was a change in command ceremony. The whole company lined up, orders were read, and it became official that I became the commanding officer of Company A 15th Medical Battalion.

When I took over command I informed the troops that, in honor of the change of command, we were going to take a run. Sure enough, we all took off and ran the circle around the huge helicopter area. It was about a two-mile run. I wanted to let the troops know that they were dealing with somebody who was more than capable of doing what they had been trained to do. I was fit and ready to serve. My extensive training prepared me to be the most highly trained physician among the four that were assigned to the unit. I was prepared for duty, present and accounted for.

After assuming command, I noticed that the executive officer and the first sergeant had overlapping responsibilities, which was causing some friction. I didn't know what I was doing, but I knew this tension had to stop. I called both of them into the office.

We sat there and chatted for a few minutes, and then I finally said to them that we had to work like a team. Any friction between the two of them would have to cease immediately. I also told them that if it didn't stop, one of them would end up at the headquarters company. That really got their attention. As of that moment, they worked perfectly together, and they worked perfectly with me. I was functioning completely by instinct, but it worked.

After about two weeks I got called to the battalion commander's office area, and he informed me that our company was going to move out to an area called Landing Zone Hammond, which was about 80 travel miles away. This would be the landing zone for several battles that were taking place at the base of the Phu Cat Mountain Range. He made it clear we would be very busy.

CHAPTER 8

The Day I Met My Friend— Who Was Supposed to Be My Enemy

On October 27, 1966, about two months into my tour, a helicopter gunship arrived on the helicopter pad at our base camp. It was carrying a North Vietnamese soldier who had been shot in the right arm.

The medics went out to the helicopter, brought him in on a stretcher, and put him right on the ground in front of the receiving tent.

He was emaciated and dehydrated. His right arm was rotting all the way from his elbow, through his forearm, and down to his hand. The tissue was completely black. I could see the fractured bones of his forearm because so much tissue had rotted away.

He was extremely weak and looked as if he hadn't eaten for days. I ordered that he be given pain medication, 25 million units of IV penicillin, and immediately started on IV fluids. I also ordered that he be given a couple of units of packed red blood cells since he was severely malnourished, dehydrated, and anemic.

I couldn't understand how the patient was awake and alert. He was speaking to the interpreter assigned to us from the South Vietnamese Army. He explained to us that he was a member of the North Vietnamese Army's 18th Regiment, which was part of the Yellow Star Division of the North Vietnamese Army. He told us he was twenty years old and he was a supply runner, not a soldier. Some of us were skeptical, assuming he was playing down his role in order to get better treatment. But he didn't understand that whoever showed up on my table was treated with dignity and respect. It didn't matter what they did, it didn't even matter what side of the war they were on. This man was a human being created in the image of God, and I was going to give him the best care I could.

He continued speaking to us through the interpreter and reported that he was on his way to get supplies when he was shot and fell into a river. He said he'd been lost and alone, trying to survive, unable to find his unit. He wasn't really sure how long he'd been out there.

From what I could piece together, he was shot in the arm,

fell into a river, and floated downstream. Apparently, he hid in a rice barn and was able to get some nourishment during some period of time, which I believed to have been about two months. He told us it was several days, but it had to have taken several months for his arm to look the way that it did. He finally waved down a US helicopter gunship because he was starving to death. The gunship picked him up and dropped him off on our medevac helicopter pad.

I admitted him to the ward under the care of Roger Gifford, who was his main physician during his stay at our company area. Shortly after admitting him, I made the decision to amputate his right arm just above the elbow. He had developed gangrene, and the arm was in such terrible shape that there was simply no way to save it.

His recovery was routine except for some separation of the skin area at the amputation site; however, it did heal well secondarily. The medics in the company developed a special relationship with him. His name was Hung Nguyen, but everyone on the base affectionately called him "Charlie."

We all took good care of him, and when he was healed enough to walk around, he helped take care of the children on the ward. He washed their clothes, played games with them, keep them company, and generally tried to cheer them up. He had a special affection for the children, as did we. So many of them had been separated from their parents and were dealing with burns and other serious injuries.

Charlie was scared because he initially assumed that we would turn him over to the South Vietnamese authorities. When that happened, he would either end up dead or in a prison camp somewhere. However, once he realized we weren't going to turn him over, he began to trust us more and took it upon himself to help us out with the Vietnamese patients.

The medics started teaching him some basic medical skills so he could help with things like IVs and injections, dressing wounds, and administering medications. He was more than eager to help out with this, and this further endeared him to me and the troops.

Every once in while, the field troops would get a break and have something called a "stand down." They would come out of the field into the landing zone area, where they were treated to a hot meal and a couple of beers.

I wanted to treat the field troops, and I had an idea. We were able to scrounge up a broken-down three-quarter-ton pickup truck. We worked on it for weeks and had it completely repaired. We put it on top of the mountain, where the communication systems were for our landing zone.

The truck had a huge bed, which was typically used for 50-caliber machine guns, and it was also equipped with a powerful generator that allowed it to be used as a communications system.

From time to time we would strip off the machine guns

and use the generator for refrigeration and send the truck to Quy Nhon, where we would buy pallets of soft drinks for a nickel a can. We brought pallets out to the forward area, set up a little store, and Charlie became the shopkeeper. When the troops would come in for a stand down, he would sell them an ice-cold Coke for a dime.

We subsequently accumulated about $4,000 in funds that weren't accounted for. We didn't feel right pocketing that kind of money; it had to be spent on the troops.

So my executive officer, Bill Boyd, and the battalion executive officer flew to Okinawa, purchased tin and plywood with the money, and convinced the Air Force to fly it back to Vietnam.

One day we received a Telex from Bill stating that we needed to have a 1-ton truck sitting on the tarmac in Quy Nhon by ten o'clock that morning. As soon as the plane landed, all the lumber and tin from the plane was offloaded onto the 1-ton truck.

The truck was driven back to the base camp, and the building materials were dropped off at our company area. These building materials were used to build hooches for the troops so that when they came into base camp, they would have proper buildings to live in rather than the tents.

Thanks to Charlie and our entrepreneurial spirit, we made a difference. We made our troops a little more comfortable. It's amazing what can happen in the middle of the chaos of war. I believe this project helped Charlie feel like his life could have meaning and purpose after the war.

Not everyone was so blessed. On February 13, 1967, a large battle took place involving the 1st Cavalry along with a group of South Korean soldiers and the South Vietnamese Army's 22nd Division. The purpose of the battle was to draw the enemy away from the northern portion of the Binh Dinh Province.

The South Vietnamese soldiers were eliminating the caves and tunnels that had been infiltrated by the North Vietnamese Army.

The 1st Cavalry troopers met up with many North Vietnamese hiding in ditches and wells. The engineering battalion was also there to assist.

One night, a soldier was brought in by medevac. Turns out that it was the captain of the engineering company that built our helicopter pad when we arrived at LZ Hammond in September 1966. The engineering battalion were sealing the caves by detonating explosives at the openings. The captain had gone into a cave to warn the troops to come out before the engineers detonated the explosives. While he was in there, he sustained a gunshot wound to the chest. By the time he got to me, his breathing was very shallow. He was unconscious and in severe shock.

It was clear to me that the gunshot wound to the chest had struck major blood vessels going into or coming from the heart, and he died.

This captain was a great help to us when we first arrived at LZ Hammond. In addition to building the helicopter pad, he also built a structure for our receiving tent made out of 12 x 12 lumber, giving the area very strong support. With his help, we were able to place sandbags surrounding this tent practically as a wall. We built a wall there that was two layers thick. Because of him, the receiving tent was a safe place to be when we sustained incoming mortar rounds. Losing him was a tragic moment for us all.

After this battle, LZ Hammond was dismantled. We returned to base camp, where our company area had been undergoing significant construction. In addition, Quonset huts were constructed as new wards for our company medical area at the base camp.

On April 1, 1967, the division changed command. Major General John J. Tolson became the division commander. He was a paratrooper, aviator, and a career soldier of thirty-one years, and he had been instrumental in developing the division before we came to Vietnam.

When he assumed command, there was a change in command ceremony. I still have a photograph of him giving me my first Bronze Star at that change in command ceremony. The ceremony always included the commander acknowledging his troops by giving them medals, and I was one of the honored recipients.

CHAPTER 9

Finding a Home For Charlie— And My Bearings as a Leader

Unfortunately, Charlie's stay on our base was rather short-lived. All things must change, and one day my forward command changed. The new commander was a West Pointer, and he was a bit arrogant. The first sign was when he first arrived he complained to the cooks that he didn't like the food they were making for him.

I went to his number two man and said, "Look, these cooks get up at four o'clock in the morning, and they cook for the patients and the troops and the officers. They're not here to cook just for the base commander. How about you bring a warrant officer to the forward area and let him cook the meals that the colonel desires."

In the mess tent, everyone ate together. But when the colonel arrived, he set up his own private table for himself and his people. They all sat together and complained about the food.

I couldn't continue to stand by and let this happen. It was damaging morale. Then one day, I had an idea. I spoke to his number two man and suggested that they could put up a small tent down by his command tent, put a table in there, and they could eat by themselves in private. The colonel liked that because it was even more private and exclusive. All was well after that.

Then one day he called me up to his tent. When I arrived he said, "Axelrad, I hear you have an enemy soldier down there." And I said, "Yes, sir."

He said, "You have forty-eight hours to get rid of him." He was the boss, and I wasn't about to debate with him.

I was a good soldier. I had no anxiety about it, honestly, and I had no problems with resolving the issue quickly. I respected orders. I saluted the colonel, did an about-face, and went back to the company area. He was the commander and there was no discussion.

I had an idea. I went to the medevac helicopter captain and told that him I needed to get back to the base camp and I was taking Charlie with us. He flew us back there without reservation. When I arrived at the base, I called my company area and got a

Jeep, and we drove Charlie to Anh Khe, a small city about five miles from the base.

During our stay at the base camp, we had set up a medical clinic to serve the local Vietnamese people. The clinic was staffed by the local Vietnamese, along with support from a rotating group of US Army medics that would come from the base.

I asked the chief medic to find a position for him. Charlie had developed some basic medical skills during his stay with us. So, the chief medic created a position from him as a clerk; it came with food and lodging. I felt a deep responsibility to make sure Charlie was going to have a roof over his head and food to eat. I don't think it was great food, but it worked well enough.

Several weeks later, I was called to a planning meeting and was told that the medical company was going to go with the 8th Engineering Battalion and a brigade of troops to the Duc Pho area. There was an urgent situation, and the Marine troops had to be moved. This area had effectively been controlled by the communists for more than ten years. The Marines failed to stabilize the area and needed urgent help.

For years, the Viet Cong and its political arm of the South Vietnamese Communists, the National Liberation Front (NLF), had increased their power by political indoctrination, torture, and terrorism to get a well-developed infrastructure. The Marines lost a half a battalion of troops—about 750 men, so they moved us up there to support the troops.

The company was organized to travel north. We were in two aircraft. I was in one aircraft with my Jeep and some other equipment. We flew north and landed at the destination point. The other aircraft developed some type of a mechanical problem and had to fly south to Saigon with all the communication equipment on board.

So that left the rest of us at the new landing zone without any communication equipment. As a result, the first night we were there, we were essentially isolated. We all knew that the enemy knew we were there. I still remember the feeling of fear and abandonment.

The Marines had already moved out. There were only a few Marines left who were cleaning up the area. So I looked around at my troops and simply said, "Look, the best thing you can do is surround yourselves with sandbags, go to sleep, and don't worry about it." There was nothing else to do. We were up there alone. That was a scary night, to say the least. No lights, just sleeping out in the middle of a field. None of us slept that night.

The next day, the other plane was repaired, left Saigon, and flew north to meet up with us at the landing zone. We were relieved to have communication equipment that put us in contact with the others. In fact, this equipment was so much better than our previous equipment, we could even call the United States. I called home. It was completely surreal talking to my mother on the phone from a landing zone in the middle of Vietnam.

Before leaving the area, the Marines had put all their trash and other disposable equipment into holes that they had dug. Unbeknownst to us, they also buried hand grenades and other explosives into the trash holes. When we started burning the trash, the piles started to explode. Several of our troops were killed by those explosions.

It is interesting to note that there were twenty-two deaths while we were there, and eleven were non-hostile, accidental deaths. One of the non-hostile deaths occurred as a group of guys were having dinner. One guy was sitting next to another guy with his rifle in his arm as he was eating. The rifle accidentally went off, shot the guy next to him, and killed him.

There was also a helicopter crash that we all saw out in the valley. The flight surgeon from that helicopter battalion decided to fly out on that helicopter to investigate an area where it was suspected that some Viet Cong were setting up camp. It was a big mistake on his part. There was no need for him to go out there.

As they were flying out there, one bullet came through the aircraft, struck him in the head, and killed him instantly. I remember pronouncing him DOA (Dead On Arrival) and signing the death certificate.

That's the only physician I'm aware of who died during my tour of duty. It gave me pause and made me realize that, although I was there to help people, I shouldn't allow myself to entertain any illusions that I wasn't the enemy. I had to remember that I was a target.

The division also needed to build several airstrips. This landing zone was called LZ Montezuma. The 8th Engineering Battalion had begun reconnaissance of the area to build airfield sites. Over two days, thirty-one pieces of very heavy engineering equipment weighing over 200 tons was airlifted into Duc Pho. They used flying crane helicopters along with Chinook helicopters to move the equipment.

The construction continued throughout the night by floodlights. By midnight, six hours after the work began, twenty-five percent of the airstrip had been completed. The engineers built three airstrips that would take large fixed-wing aircraft.

The reason the 1st Cavalry was called in was because, at that time, the Marines needed our Huey helicopters to pick up the wounded. The Marines only had these very old, slow helicopters that were used to transport machinery. Their little helicopters flew slowly and made a lot of noise. They were dangerous to fly into a zone that was under enemy fire, and they were regularly shot down. The Marines did not have good medical support or good hospital support, so we served an important function.

The 1ˢᵗ Cavalry was totally equipped to deal with these situations, and the mission, dubbed "Operation Lejeune" was accomplished within three weeks and was unique in many ways. First, the deployment of the 2ⁿᵈ Brigade to the 1ˢᵗ Corps Tactical Zone was the first commitment of any large US Army unit in that area. Second, and more importantly, the engineering effort including the lifting of thirty tons of equipment to build two tactical fixed-wing airstrips in the matter of a few days, was unparalleled in Army Engineering history. Finally, the demonstrated "Fire Brigade" reaction capability of deploying a large task force in a day and a half to an entirely open and new area of operation proved the flexibility of the air mobile concept.

As a result of Operation Lejeune, the 1ˢᵗ Cavalry left behind two airstrips, an impressive line of communications, several critical connecting roads, and a damaged Viet Cong infrastructure. In light of the limited mission, Operation Lejeune was an unqualified success.

This area was originally under the control of the Marines in the 1ˢᵗ Corps area. Since they arrived in 1965, the Marines did not want any army divisions in their 1ˢᵗ Corps area, and this was the first time that an army unit went into the I Corps area successfully.

The Marines were sent to Vietnam very poorly equipped. They were originally sent with M-14 rifles, which went back to the

Korean War. They did not get the M-16 rifles until much later.

We were there exactly three weeks, and then the medical company and the other units were moved back to base camp. Some were assigned to a new landing zone. In June of 1967, after Operation Lejeune was over, I was at the landing zone listening to my shortwave radio. They were reporting about another war. A major war in Israel. A war the Israelis won in six days.

CHAPTER 10

Foxholes and Fear

The war in Vietnam was quite complicated. Not long after I arrived, I noticed that when the troops moved out to the camps forward, the Vietnamese women would come up to the perimeter to sell us candy and things.

In retrospect, I discovered that they were counting their steps as they walked to the perimeter. Their step count estimated the distance from the perimeter to the inside of the base where the troops were. They were mapping the landing zone for later mortar attacks.

In late summer of 1967, we had just moved to a new forward camp and set up our field hospital. The whole camp was around a big hill, a thousand feet up. On top of the hill were guns. In fact, the higher-ups finally confiscated the three-quarter-ton truck we had acquired from base camp for our Coke stand and mounted five 50-caliber machine guns on the back of it.

Using the truck, they would select a zone and fire at it, so the local people would know to stay away from the perimeter. Every day they would randomly select a different zone to target, so it kept the enemy guessing.

In that routine, we became familiar with the sound of outgoing mortars and gunfire. When the rounds were going out, we heard one sound, *boom*. Eventually, we trained ourselves to sleep through the outgoing booms.

Unfortunately, we also learned the sound of incoming rounds. When the rounds were coming in, we heard two sounds. It was a *wah-whoom*. We weren't there three weeks when one night I was sleeping, and all of a sudden a round hit the ground *wah-whoom*.

The first sergeant and I were sound asleep in the same command tent. My eyes opened. His eyes opened. We looked at each other for a split second, and we hit the back door at the same time because that was where our foxhole was.

That night, about seventy rounds of mortar flew into the camp. About sixty-seven guys were moderately to severely wounded, and four guys got killed.

After the attack, we found out what had happened. The guys in the motor pool area, which was right next to us, were changing a tire and they kept the lights on. So the enemy zeroed in on those lights. I discovered that every guy that got injured or killed was running to his foxhole. The guys who got killed suffered a direct hit. They never knew what hit them.

After that, I made a decision. I told the first sergeant, "Get the guys to dig down in their tents and make foxholes right there, about two feet down." I figured that way if they were asleep on their cots at ground level, when the rounds started coming in all they had to do was roll off their cots into their foxholes and just stay there. If they got a direct hit, it wouldn't matter anyway—there's nothing they could do about that. But if they get a hit next to them they'd be okay. The explosions from mortar rounds go up and out, not lateral. You could be right next to one, and as long as you're not at ground level, you wouldn't get injured because of the way it sprays out.

The idea worked. It was so successful that it spread to all the other medical companies. They gave me the Bronze Star for that. I kept my men safe, and we were able to care for the wounded, too.

There was another medical company that was supporting a different battalion, and one night a Viet Cong or somebody got into the camp and set off the ammo dump. They always put the medical unit right next to the ammo dump. This is just the way it is set up for the support command. They put the motor pool and the medics closest to the ammo dump. Anyway, the ammo went off for about ten hours, but they had dug foxholes next to their cots like we did—they didn't have a single death. Their only injury was a guy who broke his kneecap falling off his cot into his foxhole.

CHAPTER 11

Taking Care of Our Patients

In October 1966 I was able to get to Nha Trang for Yom Kippur. When I returned, I learned there was another operation in process. It was called Operation Irving. It began on October 2, 1966, and finished on October 28, 1966.

The operation was launched by the troops of three countries; a combined force of American soldiers, South Vietnamese soldiers, and South Korean soldiers. We were told that the mission was established to entrap Viet Cong soldiers who were fleeing from the previous battle. The mission was to trap the enemy in a pocket between a group of hills and the coastline in Binh Dinh province.

The operations were complicated by heavy concentration of civilians living in the area where the troops were engaged. I can tell you that, from our side at least, great care was taken to minimize civilian casualties.

The enemy was effectively trapped by these combined forces and about 2,000 enemy troops were killed. However, they also captured 2,071 North Vietnamese Army and Viet Cong troops. This was an unusually large number of captured soldiers for our operations in Vietnam.

On top of this, I am told that the Korean soldiers went up into the top of the hills and rather than select out the enemy forces alone, they simply brought everybody out of the hills, including civilians.

The South Korean forces were considered to have the sharpest, most disciplined forces in South Vietnam at that time. The support commander asked me and one of my sergeants to go to the compound where the captured troops and civilians were located. We needed to properly care for injured captured troops and civilians. And so we did just that. We did our normal triage and made sure that everyone got the care they needed.

Those civilians who were released from our care first checked in at what was essentially a registration desk, then we would allow them to return to their homes in the hills.

Among those who were in that small makeshift field hospital, several Vietnamese soldiers and civilians with significant injuries were evacuated to larger hospitals. Once those people were removed to better facilities, we did not have much more to offer than the medics already stationed there, so we returned to LZ Hammond on the same day.

Almost every morning there were many innocent civilians—both men and women—who were brought into the company area after being injured on the highway by booby-trapped bridges or roads.

Since the Vietnamese did not have any hospital facilities outside of the major cities, when these civilians had severe injuries we would tag them as Viet Cong so they would end up at the American hospital for treatment. The international laws of war (as ironic as that sounds) were such that we always took care of captured enemy soldiers, which I felt was the right thing to do anyway. Tagging these injured civilians as Viet Cong was the only way to get them proper medical care. It was the only way we could help them.

Once they were released from the hospital, they could return to their cities or villages and get on with their lives. As doctors, we always assumed the non-combatant injured would be grateful for our help and at the very least be less likely to turn against us later. At least that's what we hoped.

CHAPTER 12

Children of War

During the month of October 1966, there were quite a few children brought into the company area, usually by helicopter. These children suffered everything from burns to shrapnel wounds to severe trauma, like severe head injuries and losing limbs.

One particular twelve-year-old boy had the tip of his finger damaged, and I had to do a full-thickness skin graft to cover the defect.

One child brought to us had been hanging around where the trucks dumped trash. A truck had backed into this boy and completely separated his sternum from his ribs. When he came into the company area, he was turning blue (a condition called cyanosis). The reason for the cyanosis was that when he inhaled, his sternum would depress into his chest and prevent his lungs from filling.

I had just read in the military manual about the treatment of this problem; I simply made an A-frame on the stretcher and, with the boy under local anesthesia, used towel clips to lift his sternum onto the A-frame. The child immediately began to lose his cyanosis. At that point, even though he was having pain, he was very stable. He was evacuated to the army hospital in Qui Nhon.

One day, the medevac helicopter brought a young girl to our receiving area, and she was probably about ten years old. She had either stepped in front of a mine or suffered gunshot wounds; whatever the cause, both of her arms and one of her legs were blown off. She was stabilized, given blood and antibiotics, and subsequently transferred to the evac hospital in Qui Nhon for further treatment.

We also had a significant number of children brought in by the helicopters who had been separated from their families. We never knew where their parents were. It was heartbreaking.

One day a boy of about eleven or twelve was brought in by medevac. He was in rather severe congestive heart failure. He had such a bad heart murmur that you could practically see his chest vibrating from the murmur. As a complication of his congestive heart failure, his liver was down to his belly button. We placed him on the medical ward and gave him medications to improve the heart failure and to help him get rid of the excess fluid. One of the physicians, Roger Gifford, was on the ward, and we decided to take him to the evac hospital in Qui Nhon, where he would see the cardiologist in consultation. So, Dr. Gifford and I flew with the boy down to the hospital to consult with the cardiologist.

The cardiologist at the hospital confirmed that he had a very significant and severe heart murmur from a congenital heart defect, and this would require open-heart surgery, which they were unable to perform at that hospital. So we took him back to the landing zone, feeling dejected that we might not be able to help him.

However, after making several calls around the ranks via radio, we discovered that there was a chest surgeon on the Navy hospital ship, USS Repose, which was off the shore of Chu Lai supporting the Marines in the area. This was located significantly north of our position.

We sent a Telex to the ship to get permission to take the young boy to the chest surgeon located in that hospital; they replied, requesting that we get permission from his parents.

We obviously did not know where his parents were located, so I flew to Qui Nhon and got permission from the province governor. He gave us a written document giving permission for surgery with the understanding that if the boy died on ship, he would be brought back to Vietnam to be buried.

I created orders that allowed Gifford to take the boy north to the ship, and the ship accepted the authorization from the province governor. The chest surgeon attempted to correct his heart problems, but the boy died on the operating table. The ship was on its way to Okinawa to be resupplied and then was returned to Vietnam.

Instead of burying him in Vietnam, as originally intended, the ship command decided that they would have to bury him in Okinawa. So, to this day that boy's parents (if they're still alive) probably have no idea what happened to him or that he is buried in Okinawa. It's a really sad thought. I still have those documents from the ship as well as from the province governor. We did all we could to save that boy's life.

There were also many children with significant skin burns. We kept all these children at our company area for treatment until they recovered. Then we'd find homes for them, since we had no idea where they came from and really no means of locating their parents.

It was these children that Charlie so lovingly cared for. I now realize that even though we were his "enemy," he knew he was achieving his own victory by helping his people, even if it was with our help. Caring for the children superseded all concerns of assisting enemy soldiers—for us and for Charlie.

CHAPTER 13

Medicine in the Trenches

Whenever someone needed to be evacuated from our field hospital to a real hospital, we would call the Dustoff helicopters to fly out to pick up the wounded.

The chain of medical care was this: Our battalion always picked up our own wounded with our own medevac helicopters and brought them from the battlefield back to the landing zone. As soon as we stabilized them and gave them the necessary treatment in the receiving tent, we would call the hospital in Quy Nhon. They would send a Dustoff helicopter to pick them up.

The difference between our helicopters was that the medevac helicopters were armed. There were two 50-caliber machine gunners on those helicopters, one on the right and one on the left. When they went out for a pick-up, they could at least protect themselves.

By contrast, the Dustoff helicopters were not armed, nor did they have gunners of any kind. So, needless to say, once you were in one of those Dustoff helicopters you'd better not fly over any major hostilities.

During the time we were at that landing zone, there were other medical problems we had to deal with. One soldier came in with leeches attached to him—there must have been at least fifty leeches on him. After removing the leeches, we placed them in a cup of alcohol. This caused the leech to contract, and you could see the significant amount of blood that the leech had consumed.

Also during that period of time, the physicians all became experts in parasitic disease as well as malaria. We had examples of tapeworm, roundworm, and many other parasitic skin infections.

There was one Vietnamese patient, an elderly gentleman, who was injured and starved, and his skin was covered with lesions related to parasitic infections. These are things we never would have seen being trained in the US and, honestly, even to this day most physicians in the US have never seen a serious case of parasitic infection.

On one occasion, two soldiers were brought in because they were bitten by local animals, which were usually monkeys. When a trooper came in having been bitten by one of these animals, there was automatic rabies board review.

The rabies board was back at base camp, and we would have to evacuate them to the base camp, where they would decide who would get rabies injections. A decision had to be made because the rabies infection itself was lethal.

I recall the rabies board determined those two soldiers were to be transported to Quy Nhon hospital for rabies treatment. They were placed on an aircraft that was evacuating several other patients.

Just after takeoff, the pilot of the aircraft did not respond correctly to the ground controller. He turned left instead of right, and he flew the plane directly into Hon Cong Mountain, the large hill next to our base camp. Everybody on the craft died in the crash, so the two soldiers never made it to the rabies board. To this day, the thought of watching that plane explode in a fireball on the side of that mountain makes me shudder.

There were other instances where the troopers or local people would walk into something called Punji sticks. These were small traps made with very sharp sticks. If you stepped into one of these traps it was very painful, and if they got you good enough you could die— either from bleeding out there on the spot or from gangrene later.

There were situations where the troopers would be walking in rice paddies for days and then would get something called trench foot. Many times the cases were so severe that the troopers had to be evacuated to the hospital in Qui Nhon for treatment.

I also saw several cases of something called inguinal necrosis, likely caused by a parasitic infection. The skin and tissue in the groin area, an important passageway for blood vessels, would start to rot and die. It was a horrific thing to see.

CHAPTER 14

Confronting Death

On December 24, 1966, I was told there was going to be a special visitor to come speak to the troops on Christmas Day. Since our landing zone with its secure perimeter was a safe place to be during the daytime, VIPs and visitors were often brought out to our forward area.

The next day, Christmas Day, I was told we had a special guest on the base and that he was a few hours early for his program. He would be staying in the medical area until his program started. I walked into my command tent, and there they were—the Reverend Billy Graham and his singer, George Beverly Shea.

I wish I had a picture to prove it, but I was so excited I forgot to take a picture with him. The first sergeant and I sat in the command tent for about two hours in conversation with Reverend Graham and Mr. Shea. It was one of the most interesting discussions I've ever had.

There was no religious content, but it was obvious that Billy Graham was a very charismatic person. It is my firm belief that whatever company he worked for, he would have risen to the top position. He did speak to the troops, and at least I have a photograph of that. It was a very exciting day to host the most famous minister in the whole world.

During this period of time, there was a two-day truce with the enemy troops to celebrate Christmas. Then on December 27 at about 1:30 in the morning, I received a communication that one of our landing zones was being overrun. We were to expect a large number of wounded patients.

Sure enough, all of a sudden, the medevac helicopters were called out, and they were returning at very frequent intervals with the wounded. There were so many wounded soldiers that some of the gunship helicopters were also used to pick up the wounded.

They were coming in so fast, I had to go out on the helicopter landing pad and triage when they were taking the wounded off the helicopters. There was an empty tent next to the receiving tent, and the wounded soldiers with severe head injuries or in a coma had to be sent there. They were attended to, but nothing specific was done for them. They were not going to survive.

The other wounded went into the receiving tent, where they were immediately given emergency care. When they were stabilized, we called the helicopters from the hospital to come pick them up.

The official description of these events went like this:

On December 27 at 5 minutes after 1 in the morning, 3 NVA battalions performed a surprise attack on LZ Bird in the Kim Son Valley. The enemy units through 3 fierce human waves of assaults conducted simultaneously with mortar attack equipment supplemented by, as I recall, rifles and machine guns, and they attacked the landing zone.

The attack came through the north end of the landing zone, and the area was defended by one company of troops from the first of the 12th Calvary. With that unit there were 2 artillery batteries. The North Vietnamese soldiers broke through the perimeter and occupied the gun positions, and the 12th Cav troops fought back hand in hand with everything they had. Finally some of the 105's were cranked down to point-

blank range, and beehive rounds sliced through the at-

tackers like scythes.

The weather was bad. It was heavily raining,

and 7 other units responded to assist this landing zone

in its attack. Of the original 199 who composed the LZ

base strength, 28 were killed and 87 wounded with 1

reported as missing.[1]

When all the wounded were brought in, I noticed something strange—there were no dead bodies. Then the next day, a Chinook helicopter arrived that apparently had gone out to pick up the bodies. Twenty-seven body bags were off-loaded by my medics and taken to the grave registration area.

There were four physicians in our company. We had to divide the bodies up to assess the cause of death and sign the death certificates. I signed off on eight bodies, with cause of death being shrapnel injury.

I later learned, after reading the history of the 1st Cavalry, that one of these sergeants won the Congressional Medal of Honor during that battle, and for a good reason. He saved about seven hundred troops, among other things.

---

1   Adapted from "1st Cavalry Division History: Vietnam War," *Cavalry Outpost Publications and Trooper Wm. H. Boudreau, "F" Troop, 8th Cavalry Regiment* (1946–1947), last modified January 20, 2013, http://www.first-team.us/tableaux/chapt_08/

There was such a large group of the enemy that the base would have been completely overrun and hundreds of American lives would have been in jeopardy had these brave men whose death certificates I signed not sacrificed their lives.

CHAPTER 15

A True Commitment to Saving Lives

There was a forward company of troops, or a platoon of troops, called the 2nd of the 9th. The helicopter battalion had a company of infantry troops attached to them, and these troops were out in the forward areas.

When they set up at night, they set up a perimeter, so that if anybody was outside of the perimeter, they knew it was an enemy and they could open fire immediately.

Around January 2, 1967, three of their guys went out on patrol and, as they came back to their command area, the guys on the perimeter mistakenly shot their own men. We got a call from the helicopter battalion commander that he wanted us to send a helicopter out to the area with a doctor.

It was toward the end of the rainy season, but it was raining very heavily. The wind was blowing at about thirty knots, about thirty-five miles an hour. That is almost too strong for a helicopter to fly safely.

Now, these guys were in the woods, and the commander wanted us to send this helicopter with a physician to pick up these guys who had been shot by their own men. It was a very tense situation for him.

I went to the helicopter battalion—our own medevac helicopter captain—and said, "This battalion commander has requested that we send one of your helicopters out with a doctor in it. I'm not going to send a doctor." Then he said, "Well, I'm not going to send a helicopter." He was right. You can't fly those helicopters in the woods in that kind of wind and rain. You'll lose the whole crew; they'll fly right into the trees. They just don't have the control of the aircraft. So, the battalion commander went in himself and got those three guys in his own helicopter and brought them to our company area.

Two of these guys were dead on arrival. They were shot in the chest, and they were dead. There was a third one who was shot, but he was still alive. We were able to give him proper treatment to get him stabilized. At this point, we would normally call in the helicopters from the hospital to pick him up, but the wind was so bad that we couldn't do that. So, we had to call the Air Force. We had an airstrip, and we knew that a large aircraft wouldn't have a problem flying in that wind and rain.

We called the Air Force to send a pick-up. The aircraft did not have a medic, so I said, "We need a volunteer medic to fly back with the patient." My executive officer, Captain Bill Boyd, volunteered. They flew back to the base camp, and when they got there, Bill made a risky decision.

Instead of taking him over in an ambulance to the surgery hospital in our base camp, Bill decided to call the medevac to come and fly him over there. It was maybe two miles from the airstrip to the field hospital, and a box ambulance could have been there in fifteen minutes. Bill was thinking to get the guy to the hospital quicker than that, so he called for the helicopter instead.

Once they got Bill and the patient on the helicopter, it was raining so hard they couldn't find the hospital. They literally got lost flying around in the fog over their own base camp. They were eventually able to find it and land, but they were lucky they didn't crash.

The Air Force gave those pilots a distinguished flying crosses for coming out to pick up those wounded men and take them back to base camp. So, I decided that I needed to give Bill Boyd something special for volunteering to be the medic on that flight.

I gave him a Soldier's Medal, which is the highest honor you can get in saving a life in a non-combat situation. It is usually given in peacetime. For instance, if the guys are training with hand grenades, and somebody drops one on the ground nearby and one of them takes a chance and goes and grabs it and throws it, you'd give him a Soldier's Medal. It signifies a special act of bravery.

So, I gave Bill the Soldier's Medal. But now when I think back, I probably should've given him a Silver Star or something for bravery, at the level of a distinguished rank.

As far as I'm concerned, the helicopter pilots and their crew were the bravest people in the whole war because they would fly into areas that were incredibly dangerous. They knew they were taking a risk to pick up the wounded, and they never really got the acknowledgment and honor that they deserved.

Also, the medics—people write about combat, but they don't write about the medics. They don't talk about the experiences of the medics. Those medics go out into hostile situations, scarcely armed, to attend to the wounded and try to save lives.

I'm hoping that, in part, this book will shed some light on the bravery of those pilots and medics.

CHAPTER 16

Saying Good-bye to Vietnam and My Friend Charlie

Six months later, when I was leaving the country, I went back to the base camp to pick up my personal items. While I was there, I drove to An Khe to check on Charlie and say good-bye.

The clinic had been built up nicely by the local Vietnamese and the visiting physicians, and Charlie had been trained to be a physician assistant.

When the Americans left in 1971, he was the only medic left in town, and he actually practiced medicine for about ten years. He did get married. He had seven children and many grandchildren.

Four of his sons became college graduates.

I've thought much over the years about the effect that Charlie had on the troops as well as the children who were under his care.

When I think about his time with our company, I am filled with a sense of fulfillment and accomplishment. He helped out so much with the children. It is unbelievable how many children came in off our helicopters that were cared for by our company of medics and physicians.

Most of our company members were not career soldiers but had volunteered to serve as airborne medics in the army. This meant that they obligated themselves to three years in the Service. In contrast, draftees were obligated to two years of service.

I sensed that the care of Charlie and the children created an atmosphere of purposeful giving for my troops. They almost always had a good attitude, and we had very few disciplinary problems.

Many of my company members gave me compliments when they were leaving the country to return to the United States. Several made sure I understood that I was the best company commander they ever served under.

Charlie essentially was adopted by all who cared for him; after a very short period of time, they did not look upon him as an enemy. He was trusted and respected by all.

It was after our reunion almost fifty years later, when I brought back the bones, that I was able to fully grasp the depth of his character and courage.

Orders were issued to me on August 2, 1967, which indicated that I was scheduled for departure from An Khe on August 9, 1967. I was told to report at six o'clock in the morning with my baggage.

I was to depart wearing my fatigues and combat boots and to have in my possession a khaki uniform on returning to the United States. I packed by baggage and put the bones inside.

I finally left Vietnam on August 11, 1967.

CHAPTER 17

Coming Home to History

Upon returning to the United States, I had a thirty-day leave, and then I was assigned to Kimbrough Army Hospital at Fort Meade, Maryland.

I was there for about a week when the physician, Major Ognibene, came up to me and said, "Since you're the new doctor at the hospital, we want you to go on maneuvers with the troops." I looked him squarely in the eye and said, "If you don't mind, I want to talk to the hospital commander in your presence." We went down to the commander's office, and I said to him,

"Colonel, if you order me to go on maneuvers with the troops, no question that I'm going to do that. However, you know where I've been. I just spent twelve months moving with the combat troops. I slept in underground bunkers and was involved in two mortar attacks. You have doctors at this hospital who have medical practices in Baltimore. They used some kind of influence to be assigned to Fort Meade, which is halfway between Baltimore and Washington, DC."

I finished by saying, "I think one of them should go before me. They haven't put their fatigues on since they left Fort Sam Houston."

The colonel looked at me, and within two seconds he said, "You're excused."

I saluted him, looked at the major, did an about-face, and walked out. Needless to say, I never went out on any maneuvers with any troops.

About six months later, Martin Luther King, Jr. was assassinated. There were significant riots in northeast Washington to the point that a military response was necessary. At that time, Washington, DC, was a federalized city. They had no National Guard.

I was sitting at my desk when the colonel called me and said, "Axelrad, you owe me one. As you know, Martin Luther King has been assassinated, and there are riots in northeast Washington. The base is sending an armored cav unit and is going to park them at the old soldier zone in northeast DC. We're sending a medical unit into northeast Washington. They will be stationed at an elementary school that is fenced in. You're the only one around here who knows what the hell to do. So you show up tonight at seven o'clock with your fatigues on, and you're taking the medical unit into DC."

So, I had a very interesting year in Vietnam, and then I continued my experience in Washington, DC, during very unusual times.

I received orders on June 5, 1968, to be relieved of my active-duty status. On August 11, 1968, I was discharged from the army and was given a travel voucher to return to my home of record.

When I was discharged, I flew into San Francisco. From there I flew home to Houston. My family met me at the airport.

The first full day I was home, I put my army locker in the closet, bones and all. I took my shoes off and went out on the bayou. I walked for two hours barefoot on the running path just to get a feel for the moment, to feel the earth beneath my feet.

In that moment, I clearly remembered my father's handwritten will. In it, he recorded his last wishes for all of his children to be good citizens of the United States.

I was glad to be home. And, I sincerely hoped my military service had accomplished my father's dying wish.

Finding My Old Friend and Finally Making Some Sense of a Senseless Conflict

The war in Vietnam was not lost in the field, nor was it lost on the front pages of the New York Times or on the college campuses. It was lost in Washington, D.C., even before Americans assumed sole responsibility for the fighting in 1965 and before they realized the country was at war; indeed, even before the first American units were deployed. The disaster in Vietnam was not the result of the impersonal forces but a unique failure, the responsibility for which was shared by President Johnson and his principal military and civilian advisers. The *failings were many and reinforcing: arrogance, weakness, lying in the*

pursuit of self-interest, and, above all, the abdication of responsibility

to the American people.

    —H.R. McMaster, *Dereliction of Duty*

As my sons and grandson and I were standing there at LZ Hammond in 2012, I began to think about the fact that 56,000 Americans were killed. And I survived. Several hundred thousand were injured. And I survived.

What disturbed me the most was the fact that children were separated from their parents. I remember the children who were brought in the helicopters were injured or burned. Many young were ill with several types of intestinal worms, including hookworm and pinworm, and were severely anemic. Many of the children had severe anemia secondary to malaria. Some of the children lost their limbs to landmines. It was horrific.

And I remember the young men—the troops. When they came in for a stand down, a hot meal, and a hot shower, they were also given a couple of beers. These troops were in forward areas and were completely overwhelmed with fear. After the two beers, every time without fail, a few of them would just go berserk. We would have to give them 100 mg of Thorazine to get them to sleep. When they woke up the next morning, they were calmed down and anxious to put on their backpacks and go out with their buddies, back to the forward areas. Their reality was berserk.

Looking back, the whole situation was berserk. We never should have been there in the first place. That, of course, is said in hindsight. But it's worth noting that, in the end, really nothing good came out of that war for either side.

So, the best we can hope for is that we learn from it. I hope that this book will, at the very least, add to that cause.

I remember the night we arrived in Hanoi in 2013 with the bones in my suitcase. I had to get a special letter from the Vietnamese consulate in Houston, along with a letter of permission signed by Charlie.

It's not every day that someone travels with arm bones in his suitcase. I wanted to be sure that the suitcase could pass through an X-ray machine in Vietnam without my ending up in a Vietnamese prison.

The funny thing is, when I contacted the Vietnamese consulate in Houston, they had no idea what to do. They had procedures in place for bringing human remains back to Vietnam for burial, but they'd never had someone bring bones back to a living person.

In fact, I've often wondered if I'm the only one who ever did anything like this—bring someone's bones back to them while they're still alive.

So, we spent some time in Hanoi before heading to An Khe the next morning. It was a sleepless night for me. I was eager to see Hung again after all these years of wondered if he was okay. For so long, I'd had no idea whether he was dead or alive.

And here I was, miraculously on the verge of our reunion.

I'll never forget the ride to his house. We had a driver and my entire entourage was with me—my sons Chris and Larry, my grandson Owen, Chris's daughter Jiji, and Hoa, the journalist who had found Hung for me.

We got out of the car. I looked around, and I remember the first thing I thought was, *Wow, Charlie's had a good life.*

It was peaceful out there. The path up to his house from the road was about thirty yards, but it seemed like a mile. As we walked up toward his house, I was clutching the box containing Charlie's arm bones.

My son Chris was videotaping the entire thing. We came around a little bend in the path, and suddenly I saw all these journalists and TV cameras. This was big deal in Vietnam, apparently, as the story was in the papers for weeks leading up to my return.

Hoa had also put the story out on the AP wire, so there were AP journalists, journalists from Public Radio International, and people from all the Vietnamese newspapers and TV stations.

Then I saw Hung. He was smiling that big smile I'd always

remembered. Hung was always cheerful when he was on our base. He had been through the most horrible experience, he'd lost his arm, yet his resilience and his spirit amazed me.

That moment when I walked up and he reached out with his left hand to shake my hand, I just put my arms around him and hugged him. He seemed surprised at first, but then he embraced me as well. We were laughing and I realized in that moment just how much I'd missed him.

Charlie and I walking to his home with the arm bones in a box.

As we walked up the path to his home, we held hands. He showed me into his home and, let me tell you, his home was so beautiful. I was so proud to see that. Most of his family was there—three of his sons, two of his daughters, and several grandchildren.

Unfortunately, his wife had passed a few months before we were able to get there. I still feel bad I wasn't able to help in some way. She'd developed lung cancer and died.

After some extensive media interviews and photos, things finally settled down and our families had lunch together. I remember it was like we were all family, one big family sitting together and enjoying a wonderful home-cooked meal.

I was watching my sons laughing and talking with Charlie's sons. I remember both Larry and Chris spending a little time with Charlie and, even though they couldn't talk directly, there was a fondness there.

And Charlie and I spent hours talking with Hoa acting as our translator. Charlie filled me in on all the highlights of the last forty-five years. I would like to say I was amazed at his stories but, honestly, none of it was a surprise because I knew Charlie.

He'd become almost like the village doctor after the war. He worked for the government, raised seven kids, and five of them were now college-educated. He and his wife worked hard and truly made a positive impact on their community and the world.

People have asked me many times, "Why did you save an enemy soldier? What motivated you to go out of your way to help him so much?"

To me, the answer is simple and always has been: It's what we're supposed to do. Beyond all the politics and things we imagine are so different between us, we all come from the same source, the same place.

At the time, I never gave it a second thought, and I never have since. If I was in the same situation again, I'd do it the exact same way.

There are no accidents.

Our family in Vietnam in 2013, during a return visit with Charlie's family.

AFTERWORD

The story in this book describes a religious philosophy called Repairing the World, or *Tikkun Olam*. Rabbi Isaac Luria, a sixteenth-century Kabbalist, explains that when God created the world, God sent a fleet of ten perfect fragile vessels of pure light from the heavens to the earth. These sacred vessels contained perfect beauty, perfect honor, perfect respect, perfect understanding, compassion, and judgment. But our imperfect world couldn't handle the fragile Divine perfect light, and the sacred vessels shattered.

The broken shards of light spread out across the earth. The sparks hid themselves in the physical world, and some even hid themselves in the souls of human beings. Since that moment, our job has been to repair the world by finding the shards of light that are buried in the darkest of places. When we exhibit the sacred qualities of the light, we uncover the sparks and repair the vessels—one action at a time. Our purpose is to bring sacred qualities like compassion, honor, and understanding to the chaos in the world.

When Dr. Axelrad served in Vietnam, he brought Divine qualities of sensitivity, judgment, compassion, and strength to a very dark place. When asked about why he did what he did during the war, he replied that he was compelled by a higher power to "repair the world."

Dr. Axelrad repaired the world through the power of his faith. He has the faith that the events that comprise the days of our lives serve a higher purpose. He has the faith that all that we do and all that happens to us leads us down our path. Dr. Axelrad teaches us through his aura, his personality, and his writing that at every moment, *we are being led by our Creator.* These memoirs show us, in his words, that "there are no accidents."

—*Rabbi Ranon Teller*

of Congregation Brith Shalom in Houston, Texas

APPENDICES

APPENDIX A

Photos

Riding a jumping horse at the age of fourteen.

Medical Field Service School in San Antonio, TX.

At the clinic in An Khe.

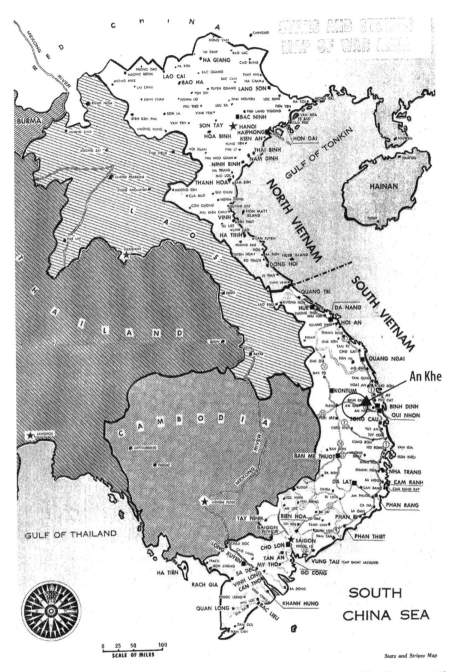

*Map of Vietnam, from **Stars and Stripes** newspaper, showing the location of the clinic at An Khe.*

An outhouse toilet on the base.

Our camp with Chinook helicopters in the background.

Weapons bunker.

Bill Boyd at the Command Tent, with VC medical kit, 1966–67.

A child with severe burns at LZ Hammond.

A Medivac helicopter picking up the wounded.

Wounded soldier being carried to the helicopter for evacuation.

This monkey bit two soldiers who were sent for rabies injections. The never made it to the rabies board as their plane crashed en route.

An older sister taking care of her sibling.

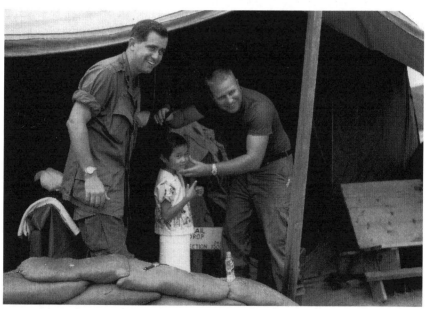

The 1ˢᵗ Sergeant and I with a wounded child.

Visiting a Buddhist temple.

Nancy Sinatra singing to the troops.

Sitting at the command tent desk.

Tag football on Thanksgiving Day in 1966.

At the An Tuc Dispensary in 1966

The receiving tent at LZ Hammond.

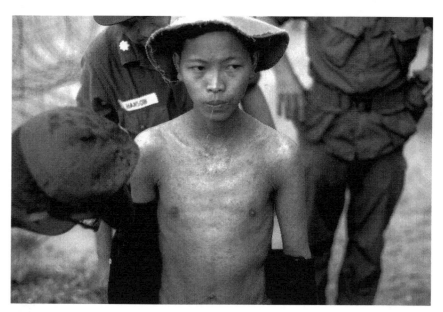

Child suffering with severe heat rash.

*This child was in heart failure and was sent to the
naval hospital ship **The Repose** for treatment.*

Sergeant Jones and I with our heart patient.

Statement of Authorization for Medical treatment.
Tờ ủy-nhiệm đầu chữa bệnh nhân.

I _Trần Thị Muôn_ being the legal guardian
Tôi quyền giám-hộ chịu trách nhiệm
of _Đặng Quốc Cường_ do hereby give permission
của vì vậy, làm giấy phép này giao-
to The United States Government to perform medical treatment,
cho Chính-Phủ HOA-KY để thực-hiện sự điều-trị, kể cả sự giải-
including necessary surgery and anesthesia of choice on _Đặng_
phẫu cần thiết và sự lựa chọn làm hôn mê
Quốc Cường, and understand that if this medical treatment
và hiểu rằng nếu sự đầu chữa này không được
is not done, the child will continue to be in extreme danger.
thực-hiện, đứa bé sẽ tiếp tục sự đau đớn đến cùng cực.
I further understand the seriousness of the boy's illness and
Tôi hiểu xa hơn nữa sự bệnh hoạn quá trầm trọng của đứa bé sẽ
will not hold The United States Government liable.
không được Chánh-Phủ HOA-KY chịu trách nhiệm.
If the child should die, I realize the body will be
Nếu đứa bé chết, tôi chịu nhận xác chết sẽ được mang
returned to me. I realize this treatment is to save his life,
hoàn trả lại cho tôi. Tôi công nhận sự chữa trị này là để cứu
if at all possible.
đời sống của đứa bé, nếu việc ấy có thể thành kết-quả được.

Signature of Legal Guardian and Date
Chữ ký của người giám-hộ, ngày
Trần thị Muôn,

Signature of US Gov't witness and title
chữ ký nhận chứng của CP Hoa-ky, nghề

Signature of Vietnamese witness and title
Chữ ký nhận chứng VN ,nghề nghiệp

CAPTAIN CAO-VĂN-CHẤN
Phú Mỹ district chief, BINH-ĐINH province

The document I obtained so that we could send the boy for life-saving heart surgery on a Navy hospital ship.

Inspecting civilians who were captured by the South Korean troops for medical issues.

All soldiers had to wash their own clothes.

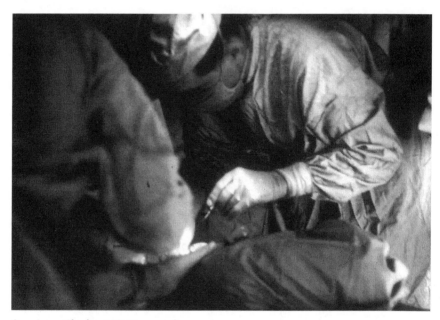

Surgery on Charlie at LZ Hammond.

Charlie and I going back to base camp.

Charlie's arm bones

Charlie and I –both aged 27–with the bones from his amputated arm.

Chris, Owen, Larry and I on tour in Vietnam, September 2012.

Owen and I, riding a buffalo.

In a rice paddy, about to attempt to ride a water buffalo.

Owen with Saba (Grandpa) at the beach in Vietnam in 2012.

*Our story made it into **Ripley's Believe It or Not** in October 2013!*

144

APPENDIX B

Stories From Other Soldiers

When the story of my reunion with Charlie went public, I was contacted by a few of the other soldiers who were there and took part in the events that surrounded Charlie's capture, medical care, and placement as a clerk at the clinic in An Khe. I have included some of their stories here so that you could learn more about Charlie and his effect on the others who interacted with him while I was there and after I left.

~

Walter's Story

My name is Walter. I was in Vietnam from May 1969 to March 1970, assigned to the 4th Infantry Division as a Medical Service Corps first lieutenant for the entire period.

My initial assignment was with the 1/10 Cav, where I was the squadron surgeon assistant. For most of that time, the squadron

145

operated out of LZ Oasis and Camp Enari at Pleiku forward to the Cambodian border. It later rotated east to Camp Radcliff at An Khe.

Soon after that I was reassigned under the division surgeon and the 1st Brigade S5 (Civil Affairs) to be the assistance team's officer in charge at the An Tuc Dispensary (Benh Xa An Tuc) in An Khe. An Tuc is an old historical name for An Khe.

Benh Xa An Tuc was the Republic of Vietnam (RVN) medical facility for the An Khe District and was the equivalent of the county hospital for that part of Vietnam. At that time, An Khe was part of Binh Dinh Province, and the Provincial Hospital was in Quy Nhon. I do not know of any other medical facility in the district.

The dispensary and infirmary had been largely built under the sponsorship of the 1st Cavalry Division and its 15th Medical Battalion as part of its Medical Civil Action Program (MedCAP) during the time that An Khe was in their area of operations from 1965 to 1969. In the few months of our tenure there, I knew just the basics about Nguyen Quang Hung, aka Charlie—that he was a former NVA soldier who had lost his arm in battle and surrendered. There was little institutional memory and a language barrier that limited any further information.

I was wary at first of a former NVA soldier in our midst, but I never saw any animosity from him and grew to fully trust him. He was always conscientious and willing to help.

Over time I came to trust and respect both him and the second medical chief counterpart I worked with, Ho Dach Ngach. In the midst of an ongoing clash of cultures and communication difficulties, they were unwavering in their dedication to the mission of Benh Xa An Tuc.

To the English speakers on the compound, Hung was known as Charlie, a nickname bestowed on him before we arrived on the scene. There was a dog living on the compound that had lost a left foreleg, apparently in an accident of war. He had the appearance of a pointer, very much different than all the other typical mongrel dogs in the neighborhood, and he was known as "Victor." Apparently someone in the past had cleverly (at least in their mind) connected them with the phonetic alphabet for "VC."

With very few exceptions, Victor would growl and bare his teeth at almost any non-Vietnamese person who came too close to him. Charlie was nothing like Victor.

By the end of 1969, it became obvious that our time at An Tuc was limited, both because of the impending withdrawal of US forces and because the assistance effort was politically unpopular in some higher circles.

Although there seemed to be support from the local population to our eyes and hearts (some said "if you leave, we will die") I was aware that it was considered an "illegal MedCAP" at the higher levels of the army, and perhaps also at the level of the South Vietnamese government. I do not know the true history of this political tension.

Seeing the writing on the wall, I requested an extension of tour and service in order to help see our withdrawal from Benh Xa An Tuc through, but that was denied. I returned to the US in March 1970 with a heavy heart and was released from active duty the next day.

After that, I had no means of communication other than by letter a few times with Ho Dach Ngach. Through his letters, I know that the Division team left soon after that.

Ho Dach Ngach eventually escaped by boat with his family, and after a long and circuitous journey finally settled in Southern California. I have long wondered about the fate of all those others we worked and lived with at An Tuc.

In particular, I worried about Hung, as I feared he would be seen as a traitor by the North Vietnamese, so it was a great relief to learn that he is alive and well in An Khe. I hope that I might learn someday that others were as fortunate.

~

John's Story

My name is John. This is a narrative of my experiences in Vietnam with the 1st Air Cavalry Division Alpha Company 15th Medical Battalion. I spent most of that time as a medic with the An Khe Dispensary, which was part of the 1st Cav's MedCAP program.

I arrived in Bien Hoa on February 16, 1967, and remained for a few days until my name was called out for An Khe.

I remember the time we had to report in to the company commander, to Captain Axelrad. I was the first in line to report in. Dr. Axelrad basically told us what was expected of us, how we were to comport ourselves; he said if there was any aggressiveness and we wanted to fight, we could always sign in to the infantry. Well, my initial assignment was to the evacuation platoon, and that consisted of doing all kinds of menial work and dirty details, and I sort of complained. "Look, I'm a medic. I like what I'm doing, and I wish I would get assigned to the clearing platoon because then I could work on the ward."

Well, the complaints were loud and long enough, so I was finally sent to the clearing platoon. The platoon sergeant was Richard Mills. He was a sergeant first class. He had been in Special Forces and, of course, he was a qualified airborne ranger.

It was a difficult time. We saw the malaria patients that came in. I gave them extra special attention, and Sergeant Mills wanted to know how come I was being so nice to everybody, and all I told him was, "I'm a medic, and I thought I was just doing my job." So, I was sort of becoming noticed like a persona non grata.

I was just a twenty-year-old kid. Apparently, he went to Sergeant Mills and told him that I was in danger. There were some people in Alpha Company who didn't like me, didn't like what I thought and what I said. And he felt that, for my safety and for the safety of other people in the company, something had to be done. So he went to Sergeant Mills, and Mills apparently wanted Captain Axelrad to discuss my situation, although Dr. Axelrad never actually came to me to discuss anything. He just went through the intermediate chain of command.

There was a very hot day I was working with another soldier from Baltimore, Maryland, a fellow by the name of Dominic. We were working on a painting detail. Quonset huts were used as wards back then when we were still in the Camp Radcliff base camp.

I noticed the four guys coming out of the orderly room, and they approached me. One had this grim look on his face, and all he said was, "Mills wants to see us." So we trekked over to the E6/E7 hooch up a slight incline, and people were speculating. I remember one saying, "Well, maybe we're all going to be line medics." And one responded, "Eff that. They had a chance to make me a line medic and they didn't." And I thought to myself, "Well, what are we going to do anyway? If that's what they're going to do to us, what are we going to do?"

Anyway, when we got into the hooch, Mills told two of the guys, "How'd you like to go on out?" That was the English to Bravo Company. You know—it's going to be a temporary duty thing. So they went out to Bravo Company.

Meanwhile, two of the other guys, who were also in the clearing platoon by the way, were told that Charlie Company was shorthanded, and at that time Charlie Company of the 15th Medical Battalion were performing their duties in a place called Phan Thiet. So those guys were temporarily sent out to Phan Thiet. That left only me, and I was thinking, "Okay. What's going to happen to me?"

So Mills paused and just stared at me, and then he got that very faint wry smile on his face and said to me, "How would you like to go to the An Khe Dispensary?" I didn't know what to say. All I knew was that the An Khe Dispensary was a place where there was real work being done to help the locals and try save lives of ordinary people. And I asked Sergeant Mills, "Yeah, well what exactly is the An Khe Dispensary?" He said, "Well, it's in town in old An Khe, and it's part of the 1st Cavs MedCAP program where we treat Vietnamese civilians. Mostly—well all of whom were from Binh Dinh province." That's the province that the Cav at that time operated in. And, well, what was I going to say? I said, "Oh, sure! You know, I'm looking forward to that."

So, a couple of the soldiers—the career soldiers—were very happy for me. They said, "Look, you're going to be out there with the people, you know?" One guy joked that I'd be right out there amongst the people and he said, "Pretty soon you'd be like Ho Chi Minh, you know?" They kind of joked about it. Jones actually took me to town. He told me to pack my stuff and get my footlocker in order—the makeshift footlocker that we bought in town that Mills took us in to purchase. He drove me out to An Khe Dispensary and gave me a very solemn look. I wouldn't say it was stern, but it was solemn. But he was warning me. He said to me, "Over here. This is as good as it's going to get. So make the most of it."

I reported to Staff Sergeant Greene. I became more or less his protégé. He showed me around. He took me through the wards. He took me through the main building where the emergency room and the pharmacy was and a little area that was set aside to do sick call, and that's when I remembered guys at Alpha Company had talked about a wounded NVA soldier they simply called Charlie who was actually saved by Captain Axelrad. The result, unfortunately for Charlie, was that he lost his right arm.

Shortly thereafter I saw Charlie, and I recognized him right away because—you know—he did have the missing arm. It was only a small stump just below his shoulder that was left.

Charlie's duties at the An Khe Dispensary were extensive, but mostly he was responsible for dispensing the drugs. He worked in the pharmacy, but his major duty really was to operate the autoclave. The autoclave, of course, was used to sterilize surgical instruments. We had to have sterile normal saline liter bottles of sterile normal saline and water to clean wounds and stuff, especially when we dealt with burn cases or we had debriding processes for certain kinds of wounds, and he was excellent. He was very conscientious. He knew his job, and I often said to myself, "It's too bad that some of the other technicians who worked in the ward that I had to work with weren't as conscientious and as interested in doing their jobs as Charlie was."

By the way, his name was Mr. Hung. And during the time that Captain Axelrad spent in Vietnam all the way up until August 1967, I believe that is when he rotated out or it could've been sooner. Somewhere between June and August of 1967, he would write checks out to Sergeant Mills specifically for the care of Mr. Hung. So he took care of him, and there was a personal relationship there.

Charlie was very intelligent. He knew science and mathematics. I remember sitting with him one time and working through some algebra problems, some geometry problems, and some trigonometry. And I was very impressed by his knowledge and what he was able to do.

Unfortunately, I never found out what his background was from up in the north or what sort of family background he had or how much formal education he had received.

Of course, he would've been in his mid-teens by the time the French left Vietnam. So I don't know particularly in the north what sort of educational system they had. But whatever it was, Charlie certainly knew his mathematics. I'll say that much.

I remember there were times when we had alerts. There were some activities in town. Probably some local, what they called *Viet Cong*, who were harassing the National Police Headquarters and/or the popular force, the PF Compound that was in the vicinity of the An Khe Dispensary compound, and I remember that night being in the main building. I called it the Grand Building. And I forgot some ammunition. There were three rounds of M16 shells that I apparently left on one of the windowsills. The next morning in the mess hall, Mr. Hung walked in, tapped me on the shoulder, and had a grim look on his face. I saw his left hand, and he was rolling the three M16 shells. Then he bounced them in his palm, slapped them down on the table in the front of me, and gave me this look of—you know— that was careless of you, and secondly I could've used this to kill you or harm you and the other Americans in the compound, but I didn't do it. So he was merciful. If he wanted to do any harm, he could have, but he didn't.

Toward the end of my tour, this was in January, we were getting pretty close to the Tet Offensive, as it was later known. We had a pretty intense attack—a mortar attack and small arms fire on the PF Compound next to us and against the 504th MP Group, which was right behind the National Police Headquarters building right across from the dispensary compound. Mortar shells were landing all around us, and fragments were actually hitting the roofs of our quarters and the ward, and we got our heads together and my eyes were straining. I was on the front porch. I was worried about Sergeant Robert G. Carney, who became the NCOIC at the An Khe Dispensary in June 1967. I decided that it wasn't very safe for me to be on the front porch, so I ran out. I dashed out and ran toward the Grand Building and did a shoulder roll. I charged into the building. The safety was off my gun, my finger was on the trigger, and I saw Mr. Hung coming out of his quarters with a medic by the name of Duc. I got to know him very well, too. He was an excellent medic.

In that split second, I recognized who they were or I might've killed both Duc and Charlie. To this day I remember that they looked at me like, "What the hell is this guy doing? I mean was he going to fire on us or what?" I immediately took the weapon and put it on safe. We walked over into the main entrance of the Grand Building to the front of the compound, and as I was watching the gunships fire rockets I just shook my head and hollered out, "What the eff? What the eff is going on here?"

I turned to Charlie and Duc. They were looking at me, and I said to them, "You know what?" I didn't even speak Vietnamese. I told them, "You know, if the rest if this effing world would just leave Vietnam alone, the people here would do just fine. You're all good people. You're all good hardworking people. You're of the earth, you know. You can take anything that's here and you can make something out of it and you can make it work." I said, "This is all unnecessary." So I guess they got the point there.

Meanwhile, Charlie was hard at work in the dispensary every day, working in the pharmacy, doing the autoclaving, and from time to time correcting me and some of the things I was doing; he tried to help me with my techniques. If I was about to violate a sterile technique, for example, maintaining a sterile field or breaking the sterile field, he got on my case, and rightly so. So he was excellent.

I remember working with an old spec-6 by the name of Bennie—he was the old man of the group. He was fifty-two years old, and he was a twenty-six-year veteran of the army. Anyway, I just got tired of everything. I said to Bennie, "You know, eff this." I said, "Who cares whether or not these effing people live or die." Bennie— he was a big man. He grabbed the whole of me with two hands on my fatigue jacket, pressed me against the wall, and said, "Look, you! You better remember this. We are medics, okay? We don't take lives.

We save them. You understand? It doesn't matter who comes in here. They need our help, and we give it to them." And I haven't forgotten after all those years. I'm sure Bennie is long gone now. He had a heart condition, and they wouldn't let him extend. He DEROSed in October of 1967. And I still remember he used to love doing sick call.

Spec-6 Bennie would talk to the people in Vietnamese when they came in as patients and say to them, "Does it hurt here? Does it here?" And then he would say, again in Vietnamese, "Oh, you're fibbing. You're fibbing." Now what he said in Vietnamese can also mean, "You're a liar." But the way he said it was like, "Oh no, no. You're fibbing. You're fibbing." So he used to joke with the Vietnamese that way. And he used to say, "I love these people here. As far as I am concerned, whatever we can do to help them, we should do it." He was talking about the medical stuff.

Another gentleman I have to mention is Spec-5 Harry. He was a pretty sharp medic. Staff Sergeant Greene said that I would be doing a lot of work with Spec-5 Nelson. He told me, "You do exactly what he says." I was a little PFC at the time, and I remember saying to Harry, "Harry, how are we going to know whether or not the people who come in here are VC?" And Harry said to me, "You won't, and I'll tell you something else. The man who asks questions dies." And he wasn't joking. I took that to mean: don't ask any questions. You have sick people coming to you. They need your help. You render it. It doesn't matter whether or not they're VC or they're loyal to the RVN—to the Republic of Vietnam, to the Saigon regime. As it turns out, I did find out somewhat later on that was the policy of the MedCAP Program in An Khe. No questions asked. People were not constrained to turn over a national ID card, for example. They didn't have to do that.

I'm certainly never going to forget Charlie. The courage that he exhibited. His work ethic. His compassion toward others even though he had been severely wounded and he had a handicap. But you know what? He took that so-called handicap and he made something out of it. He was a natural right-hander, so he had to relearn everything. He had to learn how to become a left-hander, how to use his left hand proficiently.

Maybe some final thoughts about Charlie. The year before John passed away, he and Steve, he was a good soldier. I think Steve is still alive. I lost contact with him. He was our ambulance driver. It turns out he actually spent six years in Vietnam off and on. He had to leave for six months and then come back, and as a result he re-enlisted, and he was in the army for fourteen years. He retired and left the army as a staff sergeant and became an MP. He and John made a couple of trips back to Vietnam, and during the last one when he went back to An Khe, they actually met a lady that they used to call Saigon. She was still alive, and it was a wonderful reunion from what

I heard. They found Charlie.

They were so happy to see each other. I gave Steve some T-shirts with a group photo on the back, and I had nice design for the An Khe Dispensary and the 15th Med brass and the 1st Cav shield on the front of the shirt.

Steve gave that to Charlie as a gift. I hope everything goes well, and if anybody is staying in touch with Mr. Hung, tell him I've never forgotten him. I remember the good things that he did, and I hope all is well with him. I hope he is prospering.

~

Jerry's Story

My name is Jerry, and I was the gunship helicopter pilot that picked up Nguyen Quang Hung, aka Charlie.

I've been asked, "What made you go down to Nguyen that day?"

I have to explain what I was. I was in an air assault company, 229th Battalion of the 1st Cav., and as an air assault company, we had to stay within twenty minutes of the army units that we supported. So we would take them—we would reconnoiter a spot that they would go. We'd fly them in on a combat assault or a simple placement. We'd resupply them. We'd take home their injured. We would extract them if the going got very bad.

So the day I picked up Nguyen, I was doing a log mission, a logistics mission, that probably was taking in food, bringing in ammunition, a variety of things like that. One of the things that we always could count on was we'd have a basic mission, and then we'd get another mission en route or we'd get the original mission cancelled and have to do something else.

I don't remember which one this was when I picked up Nguyen, but it was a common occurrence for us to pick up prisoners of war and transport them back to Intelligence or the ground units, you know, company headquarters, and so that's how I got the mission to pick up Nguyen.

He was so totally memorable because of his arm. Because when I saw it, I think I distinctly remember the bone showing through and an incredible smell. It was rotting off. It was rotting off so much that the gunner and the crew chief took turns throwing up in the back because of the smell.

I've also been asked, "Did he wave you down?" No, he did not. I don't believe I ever stopped for anybody waving me down, and none of our troops, nor any ARVINs, nor any of the Koreans that we picked up ever had that as something that we would do.

~

Lan's Story

My name is Lan Thompson. I worked with Charlie at An Tuc Dispensary, and when I saw Sam's reunion with Charlie on the news, I knew I had to contact him. This is my story of who I am, where I started out, and the events that brought me to An Khe and working with John Rozzell and Mr. Hung.

I was born Do Thi Lan in 1952, in Dai Binh Village, Que Son District in Quang Nam Province and not very far from the big city of Da Nang. My father died when I was very young, and I have no memory of him except that he was well known in the village because he was a blacksmith. After my father died, I lived with my older sister Do Thi Suong, born in 1951, and our mother, Nguyen Thi Muu.

Dai Binh Village is situated along the Thu Bon River, which served then as a major waterway to get to market at Truong Phuoc on the other side of the river, and it is still a major route of travel today.

In 1964 there was a major flooding of the Thu Bon River and surrounding area, and much of the village of Dai Binh was destroyed and many families were forced to leave as their homes and property were destroyed. Our mother died during that flood, which is still remembered as the worst on record in Vietnam for that river area.

Because we were now without parents, my sister and I were

sent to live with an aunt. But she could not take care of both of us, and after some time I was sent to live with my cousin who had just graduated from her training to be a midwife. In 1966 my cousin was assigned to work as a midwife in An Khe at the dispensary there, and I was to go along to help with household chores and go to the market for her so she could do her work.

My cousin had a husband who was an ARVN soldier stationed in Qui Nhon, and she would try to visit him on the weekends when the situation at An Khe allowed. While she was away on one of her visits to her husband, a woman went into labor in the OB ward. She had instructed me if anything happened during her absence that I was to go get help from Mr. Mang, who was in charge of the dispensary to come to assist the mother in delivering her child. I did as my cousin had instructed, and in the early morning hours I was running to get Mr. Mang when I met SSG John Rozzell. He asked what I was doing out so late in the compound and where I was going. I could not speak English then, so we got the interpreter to explain what was happening, and SSG Rozzell went to the woman and delivered her baby.

In 1967 my cousin's assigned time to work at An Khe was completed and she was moving to work in Qui Nhon. At that time I was preparing to return home to my relatives in Da Nang. SSG Rozzell asked if I would like to stay and continue to work and train at the dispensary. My cousin and he talked it over, and she left for Qui Nhon and I stayed on to keep working at the dispensary. I was receiving training from CPT John Pacinowski on how to properly dress and care for wounds. I continued to receive training and work in the ER.

SSG Rozzell also got me training to learn how to sew with a local tailor. I would be able to sew on Sundays, and that training provided me the skill I would need to make clothes for the Montagnard children who would come to the dispensary. As you might remember, many of them came there as orphans themselves and without clothing. Later on, an Australian doctor who worked in the area offered to loan me the use of a sewing machine at the dispensary. This made it possible for me to continue sewing and making clothes for the children and adults who came to us without any clothing of their own, or clothing that had been burned or torn at the time they had received wounds.

I continued working the same daily schedule as the rest of the dispensary staff. We would rise early and all have breakfast in the kitchen and then go to work until around noon. It is at the beginning of the day when we sat to eat that I would see Mr. Hung and then he would go to work in the pharmacy dispensing prescriptions ordered by the staff. I would go to work in the emergency room to assist in treating new patients and those who came back for a follow-up visit.

Mr. Hung and I continued to work near each other in the dispensary every day. On many occasions I would go with the staff out to other areas away from the dispensary to take part in Civic Action Programs (the MedCAPs) to serve those people who could not get to the dispensary. On those days when we had some time to ourselves, Mr. Hung and I would play badminton games, which he would win. As part of his duties, he would prepare sterile packs to autoclave instrument sets; he did it very well despite having only one arm.

When the division moved to Phuoc Vinh in 1969, SSG Rozzell took me and Kwan, a young Montagnard girl with him. It was his wish to adopt us both, but the paperwork for adoption was always delayed, and adoption was never possible. I continued to work with SSG Rozzell performing MedCAP missions to other villages, this time assisted by MACV personnel who operated in that area.

We then moved with SSG Rozzell to Bien Hoa, where he continued to work in his medical position and I now had the opportunity to improve my sewing skills working in the market for a tailor. These skills would be useful to me later when I was married and had children of my own and I could make clothes for them.

SSG John Rozzell left Vietnam in August 1970 for assignment in Germany. At that time I left Bien Hoa to bring Kwan back home to An Khe to be with her Montagnard family. It was on this trip back to An Khe that I met my future husband at Tan Son Nhat Airport. He was returning from leave following his extension to stay in Vietnam, and he was returning to his duty station. He helped me with my travel papers so that Kwan and I could continue our trip home. We kept in touch by letter from that point on.

The three of us traveled on C-130 aircraft from Tan Son Nhat with other military personnel—both US and ARVN—as far as Qui Nhon, at which time Kwan and I continued on to An Khe and he returned to his unit in Phu Cat District also in Binh Dinh Province. After leaving Kwan in An Khe, I continued on to Da Nang to visit my sister, whom I had not seen for a long time. After visiting with my sister, I returned to Bien Hoa. There I continued to work as a seam-stress in the local market, where I made women's clothing such as the Ao Dai, which is familiar to most people now.

My future husband sponsored me on a special visa to come to the United States in January 1974 to get married. We were married on St. Patrick's Day, March 17, 1974. It was a good choice because his family is Irish, and his grandparents both immigrated to the United States in the early 1900s. We now have five adult children and five grandchildren, and we're expecting one more in early June of 2016.

My life has been difficult at times but interesting, and I have met many people who helped me along the way. I remembered my mother worrying about my sister Suong and myself if she were to die and we were left behind as orphans. She told us as long as we have our honor and are not lazy we could live anywhere and with any-body. Those words have been my guide throughout my life.

I learned much about basic nursing at An Khe, about having confidence and caring to do the right thing when called upon to help. I owe much to John Rozzell and to Mr. Hung, who gave me an appreciation for his determination and efforts to overcome what might have been a work-ending injury. But he overcame all of that, and Dr. Axelrad's documented visit to him in An Khe proves how remarkable both of these men were and are now. Dr. Axelrad's efforts to make sure he had a place to stay and work and contribute helped him grow as a man as well.

I wish to thank Dr. Axelrad and men like John Rozzell and all the countries that sent their military and civilian personnel to Vietnam to help us all survive.

Lan with SSG John Rozzell

Tran Trung Duc (Emergency Room Technician) on the left, and Mr. Hung (Charlie) in the center sitting down together with the nursing staff for supper in the kitchen area of the dispensary. We all worked together and ate together at the dispensary.

Do Thi Lien and her daughter Chi. Chi was brought to the dispensary in very poor health and after nutrition and medical care, she recovered well.

Her mother was so grateful for the care her daughter received at the An Tuc dispensary, that she stayed on to help with cleaning, housework and meal preparation. She remained at the dispensary long after the 15th Medical Bn personnel had moved to Phuoc Vinh in 1969.

Her daughter Chi was also helpful to the young orphan Montagnard children learning to speak Vietnamese when they all attended school together.

This photograph shows four young girls who were at the An Tuc dispensary between 1968–1969. The young Vietnamese girl on the left is Chi (the girl mentioned above who stayed on at the dispensary with her mother after her recovery). The young Montagnard girl who is second from the left was named Kwan. She arrived at the dispensary with no clothing and was weak from starvation. The young Montagnard girl who is second from the right was named Sally Ann by dispensary staff personnel. She had been found on the side of the road suffering from severe malnutrition. She had been eating grass to survive. She, too, arrived with no clothing.

The Vietnamese girl on the right is me (Do Thi Lan). I arrived at the end of 1967 to assist my cousin who was the midwife assigned to the dispensary. During my time there I learned to sew and made the clothes we wear in this picture. I found a school for the two young Montagnard girls to attend, and Chi also helped to teach them how to speak Vietnamese. Their attendance was sponsored by the Med Bn personnel. The young Montagnard orphan girls missed their mothers (as I missed my mother) and would cry themselves to sleep every night. I would comfort them. We all looked after each other. It was Kwan and I that SSG John Rozzell tried to adopt, but as mentioned in the narrative, this became impossible to accomplish as the necessary documents could not be acquired.

Interview on Vietnam English Language Television

Interview on Vietnam English Language Television Station recorded July 1, 2014, *transcribed.*[2]

The video is also available at www.peacefulbones.com.

[October 1966, An Khe, Quy Nhon, Vietnam]

Narrator: A day in October 1966. A helicopter brought a special patient to a US military hospital in An Khe—then part of Quy Nhon. This was an unforgettable day for military doctor Sam Axelrad. A Northern Vietnamese soldier had been shot. He had contracted gangrene on two-thirds of his right arm after three days of floating down a stream. The soldier was lucky because he got sent to a kindhearted US military doctor who decided to amputate his injured arm to save his life. A year later, Dr. Axelrad said good-bye to the war and returned to the United States. He brought with him the arm bone of the Northern Vietnamese soldier and kept it at his home in Houston, Texas.

---

2   Khoi Thinh, An interview with Sam Axelrad, *Talk Vietnam*, video published July 17, 2013, https://www.youtube.com/watch?v=YQ1h9QoVvIk&feature=youtu.be.

[June 2013, An Khe, Gia Lai, Vietnam]

Over forty years later, the doctor recalled the memorable story again. He decided to return to Vietnam and give the arm bones to their rightful owner. And that was how the seventy-four-year-old former military doctor started the search for his peace of mind.

Tran Mai Phuong: Hello and nice to see you again on *Talk Vietnam*. As you've just seen in the video, you might already guess who our guest is today. It's actually former military American doctor Dr. Sam Axelrad. And he's right here in Vietnam for a very special mission because it's this mission that he hopes is going to give him closure to the war and also give him a peace of mind for the rest of his life. And we're happy to have him in our studio today to share with us some of his stories as well as his mission, and you might find some of these stories a little bit bizarre. But it's through these stories we can clearly see the humanity that existed both during wartime and peacetime. So let's welcome Dr. Sam Axelrad into the studio. Hello, how are you? Welcome to the studio. Thank you so much.

Dr. Axelrad: Thank you very much. It's a pleasure to meet you and to be part of this program.

Tran Mai Phuong: My first question that I would want to ask you is, don't you think it's a little bit bizarre to keep an amputated arm skeleton as a war memento right after the war?

Dr. Axelrad: Well, it is unusual, but I never considered it a memento of war, nor did I consider it a souvenir to be brought home. It was really something very special to me, and at the time that these events took place, the fact that I had the arm with me when I returned back to the United States at the time, it was inappropriate for me to throw it away. I just wasn't—it really just didn't even come to my mind. And I put it in my military truck and it came home with me. And I've had it since I returned to the United States in 1967.

Tran Mai Phuong: In 1967. So tell us a little bit about your meeting with Hung, who was the Vietnamese soldier that you met in 1966. What was the story back then?

Dr. Axelrad: Well, I think it was October of 1966. The medevac helicopter had found him, picked him up, and brought him in to our unit. We were really—we were considered a medical company—but we were really a forward mobile surgical hospital. So we were equipped to do anything. And so when he came in, it was obvious he was an extremely ill man. And his arm was shot. He was shot in the right arm here. And from here down, the arm was just really completely dead and, for lack of a better word, it was rotting off. He didn't have any—there was no Vietnamese hospital to send him to, so therefore, I made the decision that we would take care of him. And therefore, we did the amputation. And that's how he came to be a patient in our forward area.

Tran Mai Phuong: Now, your facility—I assume because you were an American facility—you probably took care of American soldiers. Why did you decide to take care of a Vietnamese person?

Dr. Axelrad: My rule was that whoever came off the helicopter we were going to take care of. Period. I don't care where they came from. We were a group of physicians and a group of medics, about one hundred fifty enlisted men, were all medics that our job was healing. We were not combatants.

Tran Mai Phuong: Exactly.

Dr. Axelrad: So I didn't make a distinction really who was a friendly and who was an enemy. When they came in, they were a patient. And we were obligated to take care of them as best as we could, and that's what we did for Hung. He was a patient; he was somebody I had helped at a very appropriate time. Had he not made it there at that time, he would have died.

Tran Mai Phuong: Right, right.

Dr. Axelrad: Within weeks.

[Sam Axelrad, 1st Cavalry Division] [Nguyen Quang Hung, "Charlie"]

Tran Mai Phuong: I want to know a little bit about how the relationship between the two of you developed.

Dr. Axelrad: He told that he was a backpacker. In other words, he was taking supplies, but it turned out, as I learned recently, that he was a solider. He was not just a packer but an equipment person, but he was a squad leader.

Tran Mai Phuong: Exactly.

Dr. Axelrad: And, of course, I knew then what had happened was this guy got trapped. And all his buddies were shot and killed. When he was shot, he was standing near a river. And he fell in the river, and he went floating downstream. And that's how he really got away. And now in terms of my relationship with him, he probably thought that we were going to turn him in to the authorities so that he would end up in a prison somewhere. And that we, I think the medics, even asked him to help them. And he felt very—he felt useful. He made himself at home because he was happier to be there than where he thought he was going. And so it just turned out that way until my new forward commander calls me up to his tent one day. And he says to me, "Axelrad, I hear you have an enemy soldier down there." I said, "Yes, sir." He said, "How long has he been there?" I said, "He's been there several months." He said, "Good, you have twenty-four hours to get rid of him."

Tran Mai Phuong: Oh, wow. What did you do afterward?

Dr. Axelrad: I had absolutely no reservations to what I was going to do. By the time I walked out to the company area, I talked to the medevac pilot. And I said, "Look, you need to take us to our base camp," which was near An Khe a few miles. And he flew us there. And I took him over to the local Vietnamese medical clinic and got him a job as a one-arm clerk in a little medic. And they had no reservations about taking him. And that way I just knew he had a place to eat and a place to sleep.

Tran Mai Phuong: Right. I think it's amazing that in such a period of war, in such a battlefield, there's people coming in to basically destroy people, but there's also people like you who come in to basically save lives. And think that—

Dr. Axelrad: That was our job. And my job.

Tran Mai Phuong: It's amazing. So let's go to our next question. So you brought the skeletal keepsake back to America as the reminder of what you did in Vietnam. Do you often take it out to look at it or re-member the times that you were in Vietnam? Or did you just forget about it for a certain time?

Dr. Axelrad: Well, maybe the first twenty years, I didn't take it out. But in the last twenty years, it sat at my desk. I didn't play with it. It stayed in the bag. In fact, I don't know that I really maybe took it out into until these recent times. But it did remind me. And it was—it has something special about it. And it's almost like I was keeping it company now that I think about it. Or it was keeping me company. And that's hard to explain.

Tran Mai Phuong: That's interesting.

Dr. Axelrad: There's a presence about that. It's sort of intuitive.

Tran Mai Phuong: I see, so was that intuition something that brought you to Vietnam to try to find the owner of that arm?

Dr. Axelrad: Yes, about two years ago I opened up my military trunk for the first time in thirty-five-plus years. And in there—what was in there just blew me away. I forgot that I had. A lot of documents, the little tag that Hung had was on him, I had it. I'd forgotten about it. There were a hundred slides, and I had them converted to photographs. And when I went through that, all the memories came back. And there were those photographs of Hung. when he was injured, when we were operating on him, and then afterward when he was healed. It was at that time I said, "Well, it is time to go back." And so for a couple of years, I thought about it and then planned it. And I decided I was going to take my two sons and my grandson with me, a guys trip, so it's like we would go back and visit some of the places that were the landing zones where I was and share some of the experiences with them.

Tran Mai Phuong: After you returned to the United States from the Vietnam battlefield, how did you feel back then?

Dr. Axelrad: I really didn't give it a whole lot of thought—

Tran Mai Phuong: Right. Right.

Dr. Axelrad: —at that time. Now, I have feelings about it now because I've done a lot of research. And some of my thoughts about the war today there would be a lot of people who wouldn't—in the United States wouldn't maybe like what I said. We had no business being here. We took care—I took care of a lot of children. That has bothered me the most that when these children came off those helicopters and they were separated from their parents, and their parents were not going to be found. So after we got them well—they were burned or treated or injured or had three types of malaria—then we had to find a place for them to go. And that was very difficult for me, that part of that whole war. And based upon my research—and we looked back—we absolutely, quite frankly, had no business being here. The Vietnamese people, to be frank about it, they wanted to be free of all these countries. When President Truman had opportunities, things would have been totally different; and he didn't do it.

Tran Mai Phuong: Uh-hunh (affirmative).

Dr. Axelrad: So that's what took place. And what's happened to Vietnam today, quite frankly, I'm absolutely amazed how well things have gone in spite of us.

Tran Mai Phuong: We've come a long way after the war.

Dr. Axelrad: A long way. Unbelievable.

Tran Mai Phuong: Yes. Yes.

Dr. Axelrad: It's a beautiful country.

Tran Mai Phuong: Thank you. Thank you. And thank you for coming back, for returning to this country. After nearly half a century, Dr. Sam Axelrad had a chance to finally reunite with Hung. They reunited at Hung's place right in An Khe in the Central Province Highland of Gia Lai. So let's take a closer look at this reunion.

Dr. Axelrad: When I first saw him as we were coming up the path here, it was like I actually had seen a long-lost brother. After all these years, it was so deeply appreciated just to see him and be here with him. That alone was worth walking up the trail here. It was very emotional.

Narrator: Finally, after forty-five years, Dr. Sam Axelrad was reunited with Nguyen Hung, the former North Vietnamese soldier whose arm he amputated.

Nguyen Hung: Solider! [laughter] [speaking Vietnamese]

Dr. Axelrad: He's a doctor in Botsee?

Narrator: The most important ceremony in the reunion happened right after Dr. Axelrad took a seat. He gave the skeleton arm back to Hung. They first met when they were just twenty-seven years old. Now at the age of seventy-four, they recalled memories through photographs. Hung still remembered clearly how he was shot in 1966 and received treatment from Dr. Axelrad.

Nguyen Hung: [Vietnamese] There were only two or three patients, but we stayed in separate rooms. We were not allowed to talk to each other. At first, I was considered a prisoner, so my legs were chained together. I could only go to the toilet guarded. Dr. Sam took care of me well. I lost blood, so he gave me blood transfusions.

Narrator: Dr. Sam Axelrad considers himself the custodian of Hung's arm bones over the past forty years. He decided to return to Vietnam and give the skeleton arm back to its rightful owner. Sam saw this as a mission that he had to accomplish.

Dr. Axelrad: This reunion has special meaning for me that I had a mission that really I began three years ago. And that mission was to return the skeleton of his arm to him so that it would allow him to have the ability, as he expressed it, to be buried whole. And that's just a very hard to describe feeling.

Narrator: At the reunion, Hung thanked Dr. Sam Axelrad for his kindness toward him and his family.

Nguyen Hung: [Vietnamese] The reunion between our two families is one of affection and gratitude. The gratitude is really deep, since we represent two nations once at war. But the human connection is even stronger.

Narrator: Chris Axelrad, Sam's forty-two-year-old, acupuncturist son, felt that witnessing the reunion between his father and Hung was like watching history happen.

Chris Axelrad: Two men who were good friends in a very difficult time who became friends even though they were on different sides, and I think also it's a testament to the human spirit, even when there's a war happening and people are fighting, that there's still the human spirit, the heart. Father and Hung, they had a connection somehow with the heart. And now here we are forty-five years later back in Vietnam, and they haven't seen each other for forty-five years. It's just amazing. It's an amazing feeling to see that.

Tran Mai Phuong: Let's now talk about when you returned the keepsake to Hung. So you said you were unbelievably happy to have been able to return the wartime keepsake to its rightful owner. Why were you so happy or elated during that time?

Dr. Axelrad: Well, as you know, one of the messages that he gave the reporters when they first talked to him is that he was happy to know that it was coming back, that he was. And they said, "Why?" And his answer was, "So I can be buried whole." Those were his thoughts. And the fact that he was found, thanks to Hoa, and therefore, we had the opportunity to come back and see him, meet with him, and be with him, was an amazing event for me personally and gave me a lot of a sense of very deep satisfaction that he really, in spite of his arm being blown off—I mean, being amputated—

Tran Mai Phuong: Amputated.

Dr. Axelrad: —and in spite of the experiences of being away from home, he has what I would consider a very successful life. And obviously, he married somebody—she passed away a couple of months ago—but he had seven children. And they all are doing well. And he's got beautiful grandchildren. And we had a chance to be with them. And that was—there's nothing like that.

Tran Mai Phuong: And let's talk about your first journey two years ago to Vietnam, and you didn't manage to find Mr. Hung at that time.

Dr. Axelrad: Right.

Tran Mai Phuong: And you only managed to find him this time. So let's talk about that time when you didn't find him. What happened?

Dr. Axelrad: Well, we were at the Metropole Hotel here in Hanoi.

Tran Mai Phuong: In Hanoi.

Dr. Axelrad: And I noticed that—we noticed that they did a tour of an underground bunker so we took the tour. And the tour guide spoke very good English, and she told us about the hotel, about the bunker. So I was talking to the tour guide and showing her a photograph of me and Hung with his arm when I was twenty-seven and he was twenty-seven.

Tran Mai Phuong: Twenty-seven.

Dr. Axelrad: And all of a sudden, she gets very excited, and she informs us that she was a journalist and was only a tour guide on occasion. And we just happened to be there when she was there. And after that, after communicating back and forth from the United States and here with Hoa. And she wrote a story. And it went up and down the country. That's when I think the brother-in-law of Hung saw the picture.

Tran Mai Phuong: I see.

Dr. Axelrad: And he called his brother-in-law to let him know, and that's when they called the paper. So that's a unique experience.

Tran Mai Phuong: So you came to Vietnam for the first time in the hopes of actually finding Hung, but then coincidentally, you had somebody who was willing to print your story.

Dr. Axelrad: Right, I was only inquiring of her did she have any suggestions on how I can find his family because what I'd been thinking about for the past year if he didn't survive, I would get it to his family. That was our goal at the time, not really knowing what happened to him. Then when we learned that he was alive and thriving where I left him, and he was smart enough to stay there—good decision—

Tran Mai Phuong: It's also easier for you to find him, too.

Dr. Axelrad: Right and that was—we saw a lot of the country.

Tran Mai Phuong: Exactly.

Dr. Axelrad: But that was sort of an epic moment for all of us. And we've been talking about it since then, to tell you the truth.

Tran Mai Phuong: So does your family have a role to play in your success of finding Mr. Hung?

Dr. Axelrad: Yes, I think that both my sons, my son Chris and my son Larry, and the first time with my little grandson Owen, during the communication this year with Hoa, they were very helpful and setting up this whole event—

Tran Mai Phuong: Right.

Dr. Axelrad: —that's happening now.

Tran Mai Phuong: In our studios today, we actually have two of Dr. Sam's sons, and they're right here today to talk to us a little bit about their journey with him and the process of finding Hung. So, hi, Chris and Larry. So tell me a little bit about how your father had longed for the reunion with Mr. Hung, and why did he want it that much according to your opinions? Let's start with Chris.

Chris Axelrad: Well, I think that probably when he left here, there wasn't any closure. Everything was done in a rush. And I'm sure that he had a fondness for Mr. Hung but wasn't able to really take care of him the way he probably wanted to. So I think that probably for all these years, he thought about it. It was always in the back of his mind and just wanting to know what happened, mostly probably just wanting to know what happened to him.

Tran Mai Phuong: Exactly, exactly. What about you, Larry?

Larry Baum: I think in terms of the emotional healing and just the mere fact of giving his arm bones back and to be able to share that with him through the trip last year and then finally with the closure of the trip this year, has been very helpful. It's been a bonding moment for the family. And I think it's offered a lot of healing and closure for Sam as well.

Tran Mai Phuong: That's perfect. So how did you feel when witnessing the reunion between your father and Mr. Hung, Chris?

Chris Axelrad: I was—I never felt that way before. It was such a happy moment, and, you know, I think for me it was a moment of seeing my father happier than probably I've ever seen him. I mean, I just saw a smile on his face, and the way that he walked up and hugged Mr. Hung. And then he grabbed his hand, and they were just walking hand in hand back up to Mr. Hung's house. I knew that my father had really just found a moment of peace and a moment of completion for himself. It was unbelievable to watch that. You know, it was unbelievable to be a part of that.

Tran Mai Phuong: What do you think the reunion meant to both of them, both Hung and also Sam, your father.

Chris Axelrad: I think each of them—you know, once we were there, I think it became clear Hung, once he saw Dad, was very happy to see him and probably had thought about my father many times over the years as well and wondered about certain things. And I think for both of them, it was just a very happy reunion of two—it ended up, like my dad said earlier, it ended up not being about the bones at all. It was just about a reunion of two friends that hadn't seen each other for many, many years. And I even walked up to my dad while we were there, and I said, "You know, it's funny watching you guys. It's almost like you just saw each other yesterday." The way that they just immediately started talking and they just seemed so comfortable in each other's presence, and I could see how they really developed a true friendship back then.

Tran Mai Phuong: With regards to your search for Hung, there's somebody that's definitely helped you a lot, and that's Ms. Tran Quynh Hoa. And she's right here in our studio as well.

Chris Axelrad: She's the whole reason this happened.

Tran Mai Phuong: She's the whole reason this happened. Yeah, and she's the communication officer for the International Labour Organization. Am I correct? She's helped you find Mr. Hung. She's also the translator during the process as well. So let's talk to her a little bit in Vietnamese. I'm going to be talking in Vietnamese.
[Vietnamese] Hello, Hoa. Thanks for coming. You have accompanied Sam throughout his search for Hung. In your opinion, was there a change in Sam's feelings before and after his reunion with Hung?

Tran Quynh Hoa: [Vietnamese] I joined Sam from the first day he arrived in Vietnam during this trip. He was clearly very excited. It seemed like he was too excited to sleep. He kept asking me if Hung's family had learned of his coming and whether they would be present. Sam just really wanted to meet Hung's children and grandchildren. He also inquired about Hung's health and how his wife had passed away. After Sam and Hung met again, I could sense that Sam found peace of mind. He told me that he had accomplished one of the greatest missions in his life, and that was to return the arm bones to their rightful owner.

Tran Mai Phuong: As someone who witnessed the reunion, what were your feelings about it?

Tran Quynh Hoa: It was really emotional for me. I think this is a unique story. I was born after the war, and I have heard a lot about the war and its aftermath. But this story is about kindness and humanity. I was lost for words because the reunion was so emotional. Sam and Hung kept hugging each other and held each other's hand. Those gestures are not common in the Vietnamese culture. But Hung hugged Sam for quite a while, and they walked all the way to Hung's house, hand in hand. Even inside the house, they kept hugging and holding hands while talking. Their eyes were glistening with tears. It was like they were two close friends who had not met for a really long time. It was a happy ending to this special story about the arm. I am happy that a remnant of the war could have such a meaningful conclusion.

Tran Mai Phuong: Exactly. Thank you very much. During his trip back to Vietnam this time, his second trip back to Vietnam, Dr. Axelrad was accompanied by his two sons and his two grandchildren. And during this time, they actually visited the country that was once their enemy. Let's take a closer look.

Narrator: The water puppetry village of Dao Thuc, located thirty kilometers from Hanoi, is holding a special show for Sam, his two sons, and two grandchildren. This is the first time the American visitors have watched water puppetry. Young and old, they are all amazed by the performances.

Grandchild: Stop! Hey, tiger, something's jumping over you.

Narrator: The folk art has helped Larry, son of Dr. Sam Axelrad, understand more about Vietnam.

Larry Baum: The puppets are very intricate. And the interaction between the puppets is very nice, and I really enjoyed the way they use a lot of the Vietnamese culture, the water buffalo, the fish. And they incorporate all these characteristics into it that makes it very nice and a very wonderful experience for Vietnamese culture.

Narrator: Located by Ca Lo River in the Dong Anh District in the outskirts of Hanoi, the water puppetry troupe from Dao Thuc Village has guarded its folk art for nearly three hundred years. The special thing about Dao Thuc water puppetry is that the stage is set up on a beautiful pond surrounded by trees accompanied by traditional cheo tunes. The performances feature artists standing in the water behind bamboo screens to control the puppets using bamboo sticks and strings. The show, which includes ten stories, lasts for almost an hour. Today's audience really likes it, but they are probably even more excited to go backstage and explore the puppets and stories they have just watched. This is an unforgettable experience for Sam and his family.

Dr. Axelrad: I'm enjoying the show tremendously because it's amazing to me how they bring the puppets out of the water. They are very talented, and my family is enjoying it. This is very special for me to share this with my children, my two boys, and their two children because it will—this whole time we've been here is an experience of a lifetime for them. And I hope it will stay with them, and they can pass this down to their children, and I know they will.

Tran Mai Phuong: Let's talk a little bit about your trip this time, something that's very merry. You're accompanied this time by your family, your two sons as well as your two grandchildren. So why did you decide to bring all of them here this time? We shared an experience together last year. And this was thought to me as far as I was concerned that was part one of two parts. When I told them what was being planned, they were just anxious to come with me and my little grandkids, same thing. For them, it's an experience of a lifetime. This is what this has become for all of us.

Tran Mai Phuong: Exactly.

Dr. Axelrad: And this is something that doesn't happen very—it won't happen again.

Tran Mai Phuong: Right.

Dr. Axelrad: And as long as it helps them, my two grandkids, this will be something that they'll take with them the rest of their life. And for me, that's important. There will be a time when they'll have their own kids.

Tran Mai Phuong: Memorable experiences don't need to happen a lot of times; it just needs to happen that one time and it stays with you forever.

Dr. Axelrad: They can sit down and tell them a story that they were a part of.

Tran Mai Phuong: Exactly. Exactly. So after the war, have you ever returned to Vietnam before two years ago?

Dr. Axelrad: No. The last year was this first. This is the second.

Tran Mai Phuong: And do you see any changes in Vietnam ever since the war and also from last year to this year as well.

Dr. Axelrad: Well, I was amazed at how beautiful this country is because this time we had a chance—I had a chance—to really see the people and see the whole country. And it just blows me away. It's very pleasing to me. There are four million mopeds going to work.

Tran Mai Phuong: Every morning.

Dr. Axelrad: Every morning.

Tran Mai Phuong: That's our rush hour; we have a rush hour of mopeds.

Dr. Axelrad: They really enjoy working. And I learned something new last year because Owen wanted Kentucky Fried Chicken. And so we went across the lake where there's a KFC, and he had his fried chicken. We found him a place to have a real cheeseburger. And at the KFC, there was a young man who was cleaning the tables. And so I went up to him and I said—talked to him. He spoke a little bit of English. I asked him why he was working. He said he was a student in a language school translating Chinese and Vietnamese. And he told me that he was working to buy a book, a special book, a language book. And I said, "How much does it cost?" He said, "Twenty-five dollars." So I left him a $25 tip. And then the next morning he shows up at the hotel with his book. He was so excited. So what I learned from that is that I really think the people—that the Vietnamese tradition here is that you educate the poor better than we do in the United States. Honest to God. They track them along the vocation. It was my understanding that if they don't pick a vocation, the central government will find one for you. But it's important to work help take care of each other's families, which that hadn't changed. I mean, it's a family culture.

Tran Mai Phuong: Yes. It is a family-oriented culture.

Dr. Axelrad: Family culture hasn't changed. Probably the best in the world. And so that was my observation.

Tran Mai Phuong: So, Dr. Sam, all that you've done for Hung back in the day and also during the present time, what do you wish that others can gain from this experience?

Dr. Axelrad: You know, I'm Jewish. And one of our traditions is about— we have an obligation to repair the world. All right? I think there's a lesson here to learn that when there's somebody in need, if you do a deed of loving-kindness, it comes back. And it will return to you in some form or another. And it has many times over.

Tran Mai Phuong: Let's look a little bit about your life after the war.

Dr. Axelrad: Okay.

Tran Mai Phuong: What were some of your major events after the war until now?

Dr. Axelrad: I left the service. I went into residency at Baylor College of Medicine. It happened to be in Houston in the urology division, department, one of the top five in the country. And I was fortunate to be there. And then I grew up in Houston, and I went into practice in Houston. And then since then, my wife is very special to me. We've raised these children, and it's been very—I feel very—personally very grateful for what I have. And that's where I am today.

Tran Mai Phuong: And would you consider this, the second trip to Vietnam a good closure to your years back in the sixties?

Dr. Axelrad: I think that that's very important that I have to bring it to a close. And this is enough. In Houston, I do some volunteer work for an organization called "Veterans' Journey Home." There are a lot of veterans come home with post-traumatic stress syndrome. And we have weekend retreats for these guys for them to tell their stories. And the way they tell it, it's unbelievable. But that three days of just letting it out with their buddies—it changes their whole life to do that. And I will tell you that it even, the soldiers, the Vietnamese soldiers—when your buddy gets killed, you don't forget that. It just never leaves you. It can cause trouble if you don't speak of it, don't let it go, keep it a secret. Talk to your wife. Tell her. I'll tell you one quick story.

Tran Mai Phuong: Okay.

Dr. Axelrad: One of the veterans was talking about Vietnam when his squad was burning down a village. And they were on the last hooch. And it was being burned down. There were two children inside that

195

hooch. And both of them died. He heard them crying. Now when he came back to the United States, every time he heard a child cry, he'd have to go outside the building. I don't care where he was, he had to leave the building and go outside. And he has three daughters. So when his daughters were babies, they cried, he probably had to go outside of his house. So he told that story, it was gut-wrenching. And then he sent a telegram to everybody thanking them for listening to his story that it gave him a lot of relief and that as soon as he got home, he called his three daughters and took them out to dinner. But here I can just see, I can visualize his experience at the time it took place here, in this country, in that village. And so for me, it's—this event has given me a tremendous amount of relief. And in my deepest heart, because I feel so strong that we shouldn't have been here, that all those people who died—and I keep saying for what? You've got to think about that. I have to think about it. And I just don't think it was necessary. And that's the way I am today, but in terms of these events with Hung, all I've got to do is think about yesterday, and everything else don't matter.

Tran Mai Phuong: Everything else doesn't matter. That's great. So my final question would be what can veterans on both sides actively do to basically reconcile to further understand each other and reconcile after the war?

Dr. Axelrad: I think that if the veterans organizations here and somehow some of the veterans organizations in the United States can find a way to have a common convention and have somebody, an expert, there at the convention and bring them together and let them have closure, both of them, because I really think that Vietnam as time goes on with the amount of industry that is here and how all the other countries really are designed to do business with Vietnam and all of sudden the communications between the United States and Vietnam have gotten better.

Tran Mai Phuong: It's gotten better.

Dr. Axelrad: Then they should take advantage of that. All right? It will be a big-time healing process, and the United States could be a part of that.

Tran Mai Phuong: Exactly.

Dr. Axelrad: I know some people, and I'm going to—now that we talk about it and you've asked that question—when I go back, I'm going to give some thought about how to work on that. It will be like a project for me.

Tran Mai Phuong: It's going to be a new project for you.

Dr. Axelrad: A new project, yeah. It will be, and this is special.

Tran Mai Phuong: And I'm so glad it's Vietnam-related. Your last project was also Vietnam-related.

Dr. Axelrad: Yeah, this is special. I've got some thoughts about this and I've been thinking about it this whole year.

Tran Mai Phuong: Thank you so much, Dr. Sam Axelrad, for being with us on our show today, and I'm really, really eager to hear more about your new project that's Vietnam-related.

Dr. Axelrad: Yeah, and you started it. So I want to thank you for inviting us here.

Tran Mai Phuong: Thank you so much.

Dr. Axelrad: It's a real pleasure and honor to be part of this.

Tran Mai Phuong: It's a pleasure and honor to be able to meet you and hear your stories, so thank you so much for sharing with us your stories.

Dr. Axelrad: Stay well.

Tran Mai Phuong: Thanks, you too. I think your stories are so inspiring, and I think it's a living proof of how humanity exists during wartime and how deep it can still be right here decades after in peacetime.

Dr. Axelrad: You bet. There's more to do.

Tran Mai Phuong: Thank you. Thank you so much for joining us on *Talk Vietnam* this time, and until next time that we talk, take care and good-bye.

Spiritual Reflections

In the odyssey of what is called Life, there are significant way stations along the inexorable route that ultimately are appreciated as not being so coincidental. This revelation is totally congruous with the apocryphal notion of spiritual guidance. Even in the throes of a struggle of whether to be patriotic or intentionally life-saving, is a value-laden decision which is guided.

And speaking of guided, this is tantamount to the Yiddish *Bashert*, meaning literally "from the Lord." Differing from absolute predestination and fatalism, *Bashert* is a spiritual spice that flavors favorably the important choices one makes on their personal uni-directional timeline. While Rabbinic Judaism largely embraces that gentle but invisible force of *Bashert* largely for one finding his or her soul mate, it is also applicable on a much grander scale as in this book, where Dr. Sam Axelrad is precisely placed in a foreign geo-graphic locus at a precious and pivotal moment to save the life of a young man who was an "enemy" soldier.

Biblically and psychiatrically, the strongest human motivator is Love. In fact, according to the Gospel, "God is Love" (1 John 4:16, NKJV). The polar opposite—and again in Biblical and psychiatric agreement—is absolute loneliness. "It is not good for man to be alone" (Genesis 2:18). Love for one's fellow man is the driving, live-saving force throughout this book. Judeo-Christian philosophy stresses Love for God, Love for one's neighbor, and Love for the stranger. Even if one is an enemy, and his ox—for example—falls down, the Bible commands that one must show Love for the stranger (Deuteronomy 22:4). One must not ignore and look the other way, rather, one must lend a hand.

Knowing Dr. Sam Axelrad as a best friend and colleague over the decades, I can personally attest to his living a life of *Chesed* (Loving-kindness), *Emunah* (Faith), and *Anavah* (Humility). Incalculable are the multiplicity of kindnesses he has extended to family and friends and patients and total strangers directly and indirectly through anonymous paths of giving in dollars and in kind. Only those closest to him know of his personal, unsung sacrifices on behalf of others. So many times, if he senses a voiced need of another human being, he finds a way to see that that need is gratified. In the Yiddish vernacular, he is a living metaphor of that which is a *Mensch*—a man of generous, selfless, and noble distinction!

Each reader of this book will not only be blessed by becoming more mindful of what he or she can do to enrich the quality of life for another human being, but will be ineluctably inspired to emulate the process of *Tikkun Olam*—Repairing the World—in their own sphere of influence.

Whether you see yourself as a veteran, a patriot, a parent, a loving child, a good citizen, a person of God, and/or a Mensch, you are a recipient of The Priestly Blessing given for centuries by rabbis the world over:

The Lord bless you and keep you;
the Lord make his face shine on you and be gracious to you;
the Lord turn his face toward you and give you peace.
—Numbers 6:24–26, NIV

With love and appreciation, **Rabbi Harvey A. Rosenstock, M.D.**

ACKNOWLEDGMENTS

I want to acknowledge all the medics in 1st Air Cavalry Division Alpha Company 15th Medical Battalion who served from 1966–1967. I hope all have had a healthy and good life.

I want to express my love and appreciation for my wife, Charlotte, who encouraged me to journey through the process of writing *Peaceful Bones*. When I was in Vietnam, she sent toys for the children. We parted for several years, and I thank God that we reconnected forty-four years ago.

I am indebted to my son, Chris, who assisted me in transitioning this book. We went to Vietnam on two occasions (2012 and 2013). He blogged about each trip and took photographs. We were also joined by my son Larry Baum, my grandson Owen Baum, and my granddaughter Jiji Axelrad. I encourage everyone to visit Chris's blog (Axelradclinic.com/Vietnam) to have an additional Peaceful Bones experience and view the YouTube interview from National English Speaking Vietnam Television transcribed in Appendix C.

I am indebted to Rabbi Ranon Teller, who met weekly with Chris and me. Prior to his rabbinic career, he was a journalist. He gave us invaluable guidance and editorial help throughout the project.

I am grateful for our editor, Paige Duke, who put the polish on the final version of the book.

I want to express my appreciation to Barbara Lindenberg, who skillfully created the book's style and added the photographs. She played a major role in the publication process.

I am absolutely convinced that meeting with our guide, Tran Quynh Hoa, in Hanoi was not an accident. She was the journalist who wrote the story about Charlie that ultimately helped us find him—in the very same town where I left him in 1967. She is an exceptional human being, and we are grateful to have met her.

I also want to express my appreciation to Kathy Hille, PhD, the COO of Houston Metro Urology for her evaluation of the book.

I want to thank Rabbi Dr. Harvey Rosenstock for his valuable commentary upon reading the book.

Made in the USA
Middletown, DE
09 November 2016